HARROW LIBRARY SERVICES

KV-579-751

# Discovering Hadrian's Wall

1 3 MAR 2009

LONDON BOROUGH OF HARROW
WITHDRAWN FROM STOCK
AND APPROVED FOR SALE
SOLD AS SEEN
PRICE: 50p

# Other titles in this series

*Already published*:
Coghill: Discovering the Water of Leith
Crumley: Discovering the Pentland Hills
Freethy: Discovering Cheshire
Freethy: Discovering Coastal Lancashire
Freethy: Discovering Cumbria
Freethy: Discovering Exmoor and North Devon
Freethy: Discovering Inland Lancashire
Freethy: Discovering the Yorkshire Dales
Gemmell: Discovering Arran
Henderson: Discovering Angus & the Mearns
Hendrie: Discovering West Lothian
Lamont-Brown: Discovering Fife
Maclean: Discovering Inverness-shire
Macleod: Discovering Galloway
Macleod: Discovering the River Clyde
Murray: Discovering Dumfriesshire
Orr: Discovering Argyll, Mull and Iona
Shaw Grant: Discovering Lewis and Harris
Smith: Discovering Aberdeenshire
Strawhorn and Andrew: Discovering Ayrshire
Thompson: Discovering Speyside
I. & K. Whyte: Discovering East Lothian
Willis: Discovering the Black Isle
Withers: Discovering the Cotswolds

*Forthcoming*:
Freethy: Discovering Coastal Yorkshire
Freethy: Discovering Dartmoor and South Devon
Freethy: Discovering Inland Yorkshire
Simpson: Discovering Banff, Moray and Nairn
Spence: Discovering the Borders I
Robinson: Discovering Norfolk

# Discovering
# Hadrian's Wall

DUDLEY GREEN

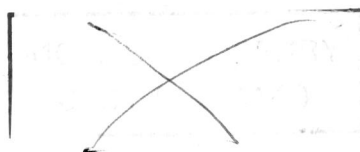

HATCH END LIBRARY
UXBRIDGE ROAD
HATCH END
HA5 4RG

JOHN DONALD PUBLISHERS LTD
EDINBURGH

*In memory of my father*

*EDGAR ERNEST MONTAGUE GREEN*
*1902–1974*

*My First Teacher of Latin and Greek*

© Dudley Green 1992

All rights reserved. No part of this publication may
be reproduced in any form or by any means without
the prior permission of the publishers,
John Donald Publishers Ltd,
138 St Stephen Street, Edinburgh EH3 5AA.

ISBN 0 85976 365 X

*British Library Cataloguing in Publication Data*
A catalogue record for this book is available from
the British Library.

Phototypeset by The Midlands Book Typesetting Company,
Loughborough.
Printed & bound in Great Britain by Bath Press, Bath.

# Introduction

Every year sees an increase in the number of visitors to Hadrian's Wall and it is the aim of this book to provide an informed guide to the visible remains. After an introductory chapter explaining the purpose of the Wall and describing some of its main features, the reader is taken on a journey along the frontier from the mouth of the River Tyne to the Solway Firth. Attention is concentrated on what may actually be seen on the ground today. A final chapter is devoted to the experiences of earlier travellers and writers on the Wall.

Although born in the Isle of Wight and educated in Somerset, I have long had a fascination for this remarkable northern monument, and for the wild and lonely country through which it runs for much of its length. Since living in Lancashire I have been able to visit the area frequently over many years. My enthusiasm has been further kindled by the Hadrian's Wall courses organised by Brian Dobson, David Breeze and Valerie Maxfield in connection with the Extra-Mural Department of the University of Durham. During 1991, in preparation for this book and in a desire to follow in the footsteps of earlier pilgrims, I myself walked the whole length of the Wall.

I should like to express my thanks to all who have helped at various times while this book was being written. I am grateful to Ron Freethy, for his constant encouragement and advice; to Colin Paterson and Keith Harwood who have read the manuscript and made many valuable suggestions; to Brigid Ackerley for providing me with a base in Newcastle and for accompanying me on various stages of my journey; to my brother Stephen for supplying numerous historical details and for his company on the Wall; to John Irwin of IPC, Chorley for his advice and assistance over the photographs; and to Jennifer Shaw for supplying the fort plan and the draft for the map. My thanks are due to Colin Shrimpton, archivist to the Duke of Northumberland for information about the Rudge Cup. I am also grateful to Mrs Huddleston of Beggar

Bog Farm, Housesteads, for providing a comfortable base for much of my time on the Wall, and to Mrs Day of the Carlisle Tourist Information Office, for her kind assistance on my visit to Bowness-on-Solway.

I would like to thank Sue Purvis of the Museum of Antiquities, Newcastle, and Maria Hoy of the Local Studies Unit of the Newcastle Central Library for their assistance. The photographs on pages 3, 6, 7, 10, 13, 31, and 140 appear by courtesy of the Museum of Antiquities of the University and Society of Antiquaries of Newcastle upon Tyne, and those on pages 18, 146 and 148 by courtesy of the Local Studies Department, Newcastle Central Library. I am also grateful to the Vindolanda Trust for permission to use the photographs on pages 89 and 92.

I owe a special debt of gratitude to Chris Haines of the Ermine Street Guard for kindly supplying me with the photographs of a legionary and an auxiliary soldier which appear on page 14. The Guard is dedicated to the reconstruction of Roman military equipment and the performance of educational public displays. Each summer they give performances at forts on the Wall. They may be contacted at Oakland Farm, Dog Lane, Crickley Hill, Witcombe, Gloucestershire.

'Verily I have seene the tract of it over the high pitches and steepe descents of hilles, wonderfully rising and falling'. Such was the comment of the Elizabethan antiquary, William Camden, after visiting the Wall in 1599. I hope this book will inspire many to make their own pilgrimage to this remarkable monument and that they will experience a similar feeling of wonder and admiration.

*Rimington, April 1992*                                      *Dudley Green*

# Contents

| | Page |
|---|---|
| Introduction | v |
| 1. Hadrian's Wall | 1 |
| 2. Wallsend to Newcastle | 17 |
| 3. Newcastle to Portgate | 32 |
| 4. Portgate to Chesters | 44 |
| 5. Chesters to Housesteads and Once Brewed | 63 |
| 6. Once Brewed to Vindolanda and Carvoran | 85 |
| 7. Carvoran to Carlisle | 106 |
| 8. Carlisle to Bowness-on-Solway | 124 |
| 9. Pilgrims on the Wall | 139 |
| Information for Visitors | 156 |
| Further Reading | 160 |
| Index | 161 |

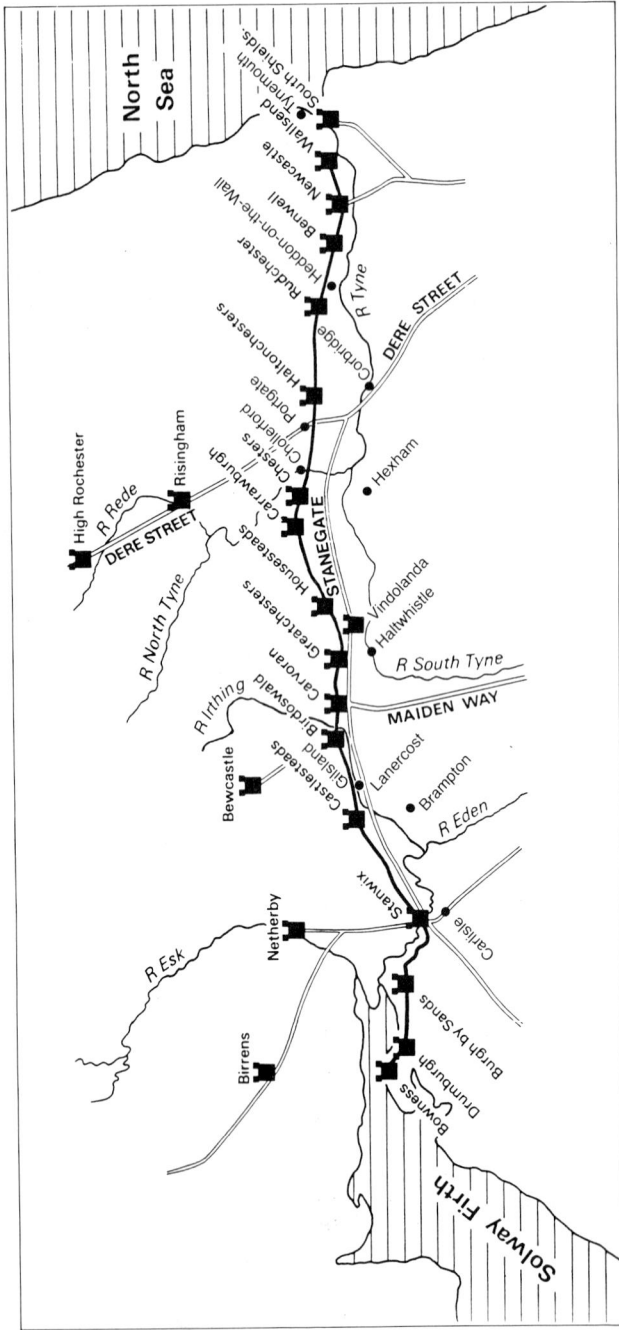

The Frontier System of Hadrian's Wall.

# CHAPTER 1
# *Hadrian's Wall*

Hadrian's Wall was an arrogant concept. For over 70 miles, from the mouth of the Tyne to the remote and lonely marshes of the Solway Firth, it provided an uncompromising reminder of Roman control. It ran through some of the wildest and most magnificent scenery in Britain and was constructed with an almost complete disregard for the practical difficulties caused by much of the terrain. For over 300 years Hadrian's Wall formed the northern frontier of the Roman province of Britain and for much of its line its evocative remains may still be traced today.

The Wall was built on the orders of the Emperor Hadrian (AD 117–138) after he had paid a visit to Britain in AD 122. In the 80 years since the conquest of Britain in AD 43 under the Emperor Claudius (AD 41–54), the Romans had slowly expanded their control over the country. The first frontier of the province had been based on a line from the Wash to Devon, marked out by the Fosse Way, a road linking the forts of Lincoln and Exeter. Slowly and inexorably the area under Roman control was enlarged. Wales was conquered, then the legions pushed north into the Pennines. Under the governor Agricola (AD 78–84) an expansionist policy was followed and Roman troops were sent north into Scotland and penetrated as far as Inverness where they won a decisive victory over the Caledonian tribes. But the Emperor Trajan (AD 98–117) then required reinforcements for his Dacian campaign (in what is now Romania). Some troops were taken from Britain and the frontier was eventually withdrawn south to follow the line of the Stanegate, the road built by Agricola to link the forts of Corbridge and Carlisle.

When the Emperor Hadrian came to the throne in AD 117 his main policy was to consolidate the Roman empire behind firm and secure boundaries. He visited various frontier areas to supervise the establishment of stable frontier lines. In Germany he strengthened the Rhine frontier by a continuous palisade

1

The Wall on Walltown Crags.

supported by lookout stations. In AD 122 he arrived in Britain where there had been trouble in the north of the province. Since there was no natural barrier in northern Britain to form a frontier, like the Rhine, the Danube, or the Sahara Desert, he decided to build a huge artificial barrier from coast to coast. Orders were given for the construction of the Wall right across northern Britain, from the mouth of the Tyne to the Solway Firth.

The head of Hadrian on a brass coin found in the River Tyne.

The frontier system of Hadrian's Wall was not intended to be just a barrier, aimed at keeping out tribesmen from the north. It clearly defined the frontier and allowed all crossings to be monitored. It was also a fighting platform from which troops could swiftly emerge to deal with any trouble in the frontier zone. In its final form it ran for 80 Roman miles (73½ English miles) from Wallsend to Bowness-on-Solway.

The Wall had several elements. Every mile there was a small fort, known today as a milecastle, and between each milecastle there were two turrets. Along the line of the Wall, or in two cases just to the south of it, were 16 forts housing auxiliary regiments of 500 or 1000 men who provided the garrison of the Wall. Immediately to the north of the Wall, and extending along its whole length except where crags made its presence unnecessary, was a military V-shaped ditch. South of the Wall there ran a road, today called the Military Way, which enabled the passage of men and the provision of supplies to the various forts along the Wall. Further to the south at varying distances from the Wall there was an earthwork called the Vallum, a flat-bottomed ditch with a mound on either side of it. Its purpose seems to have been to mark out the military zone of the Wall and to restrict entry to controlled crossing places. Some miles to the north of the Wall there were outpost forts to provide intelligence of any unrest among the hostile tribes who lived north of the frontier.

The visitor today will find few traces of the stone Wall in its eastern and western sectors. In many places the Wall has been robbed to provide building stone for the construction of medieval churches and priories, and later for the building of farmhouses. After the 1745 rebellion, in which General Wade was unable to come from Newcastle to relieve the beleagured Carlisle because there was no suitable road to transport his artillery, the government ordered the construction of a new road. Much of the Wall was levelled to provide the foundation for this military road (now the B6318). In the east the industrial demands of the city of Newcastle and its surrounding area have obliterated most remains of the Wall system, while west of the River Irthing the shortage of building stone has meant that, apart from the fort at Birdoswald, hardly a trace remains of the stone Wall. But for about 15 miles in the central sector where the Wall runs along the high crags of the Whin Sill, there is still much to see. The sheer basalt columns of the cliffs provide a magnificent natural barrier and an excellent platform for the Wall, which here survives in long continuous stretches to a considerable height. The well-preserved ruins of several forts may also be seen, and there are many traces of both the Ditch and the Vallum. This is also excellent walking country, with fine views of vast and lonely areas. It is one of the bleakest and yet most beautiful areas of the country, and the modern visitor is left admiring the ingenuity and arrogance of

The Wall at Planetrees. This section consists of Narrow Wall built on Broad foundations.

the Romans in seeking to tame and control this wild and lonely country.

The first plan for the frontier was for the Wall to extend from Newcastle to Bowness-on-Solway. The eastern section from the Tyne to the River Irthing was to be built in stone, ten Roman feet wide (one Roman foot = 11.7 inches), while the western section from the Irthing to the Solway Firth, an area in which there was much less building stone available, was to be built in turf. The troops needed to garrison the Wall were to be stationed in the forts already in existence on the Stanegate, the road which ran a mile or two to the south of the Wall.

Building began in AD 122. The construction work was done by the legions who worked in teams. Some were given the job of building the foundation of the Wall and erecting the milecastles and turrets, while others followed more slowly building the Wall. Within the first two years some changes of plan were introduced. Since it was apparently possible to ford the Tyne to the east of Newcastle, it was decided to extend the Wall four

A legionary building inscription from Milecastle 38 (Hotbank). This shows that it was built in the reign of Hadrian by the Second Legion under the governor, Aulus Platorius Nepos.

miles eastwards to Wallsend. The decision was also taken to reduce the width of the stone Wall to about eight Roman feet, and to build forts along the line of the Wall itself to house the garrison. These changes can still be seen on the ground today. There are several sections where the foundations of the Wall have been constructed to the original specification of ten feet (the Broad Wall), but the Wall which was finally built on top of them was only about eight feet thick (the Narrow Wall). There are also places where turrets had already been built but then had to be demolished to accommodate the construction of the forts. The remains of a demolished turret can be seen in the northern sector of the fort at Housesteads.

Subsequently further changes to the plan were made. A few years after construction started it was decided to build south of the Wall the earthwork known as the Vallum, in order to define the southern boundary of the military zone. A road, known today as the Military Way, was also constructed south of the Wall to link the forts along its line. Finally, some time

A model of a milecastle.

before AD 180, the Turf Wall was rebuilt in stone about nine feet thick (the Intermediate Wall).

The Wall itself was constructed of coursed stonework with a rubble core set in puddled clay. When complete it seems to have been about 15 feet high, breasted by a parapet bringing its total height to just over 20 feet. The Turf Wall which was originally planned for the western sector was constructed out of cut turves and was 20 feet wide at its base.

About 20 feet north of the Wall lay a deep ditch. This was provided throughout the length of the Wall except where it was rendered unnecessary by crags or the sea coast. This was normally about 27 feet wide and nine feet deep, with steeply sloping sides and a square drainage channel at the bottom. The material excavated in its construction was placed on its northern edge, in such a way as to provide no cover to an enemy but to add to the effective depth of the ditch.

Every mile along the Wall a milecastle (a small rectangular fort) was provided. These were usually about 80 by 90 feet. Their walls were eight to ten feet thick, with the Wall itself providing their north wall. They were probably intended to house the garrison which patrolled the Wall and also to provide supervised crossing places through the frontier. They had large gates in their north and south walls. An approach road from the Military Way provided access from the south, and in front of their north gate the Ditch was bridged by an earth ramp. Milecastles had one or occasionally two barrack blocks and could accommodate up to 50 men. Their ruins usually show traces of ovens and also a stone platform in one corner, which seems to have been the base for a flight of steps giving access to the Wall walkway.

Milecastles were constructed in two different styles and the legions that built them may be identified from their building inscriptions. The Sixth and Twentieth legions built milecastles with their longer axis at right-angles to the Wall, while the second legion built them with the longer axis parallel to the Wall. When the Turf Wall was built its milecastles were also constructed of turf, and they were replaced in stone at the same time as the Wall was rebuilt. Milecastles are conventionally numbered from east to west.

Between each pair of milecastles, at intervals of 540 yards, two turrets were provided. They take their number from the nearest milecastle to the east and are further identified by the letters a and b. Turrets were square towers, measuring about 14 feet by 14 feet inside, built into the structure of the Wall, so that only half of their area projected to the rear. They seem to have been intended primarily for observation and signalling purposes, but they could also accommodate a small detachment of men. They did not provide access through the Wall and only had a door on their south side. There is usually a stone platform in one corner providing the base for a stairway to the Wall walkway. It is thought that they rose one storey above the level of the Wall and may have reached a height of about 30 feet. In the Turf Wall, turrets were built in stone from the start. Excavations have shown that many turrets only existed for a short time and by the end of the second century AD had fallen into disuse with the Wall built over its ruins. Excellent models of both turrets and milecastles may be seen at the Museum of Antiquities in Newcastle.

At a varying distance south of the Wall was placed the Vallum. This is an earthwork of a most unusual design. It consisted of a ditch, 20 feet wide and ten feet deep, with a flat bottom eight feet wide. This made it quite unlike the normal Roman military V-shaped ditch. The material taken from the ditch was piled up in two continuous mounds 20 feet wide, which were placed 30 feet away from the ditch on either side of it. These mounds were normally revetted with turves to make them firm. The whole earthwork was 120 feet across from side to side. The Vallum usually runs in straight lines like a Roman road and is often placed at the foot of a slope, making it useless for purposes of defence or observation. It deviates from its course to pass to the south of the Wall forts, showing that it was added to the frontier system after the decision had been taken to incorporate forts on to the line of the Wall. Its purpose seems to have been to mark out the southern boundary of the military zone. At each fort a causeway was built across the ditch, which was controlled by a gateway operated from the fort. This seems to have been the way by which the Romans channelled movement through the Wall to official crossing places where they could maintain control. The only example of such a Vallum causeway gateway that may be seen today is at Benwell.

At some stage not long after its construction it was found necessary to breach the Vallum at regular intervals. Gaps were made in the mounds at either side, and the earth taken out was used to build causeways across the ditch. This may have happened about AD 140 when for a period of about 20 years Scotland was reoccupied and Hadrian's Wall was temporarily abandoned. The Vallum would then have become an awkward barrier hampering movement to the north.

Between the Vallum and the Wall was the Military Way. This was a road along the frontier linking the milecastles and forts. It allowed troops and supplies to move rapidly along the line of the Wall. It had a cambered surface and was 20 feet wide. Much of its route runs through rugged and difficult terrain and it is a fine example of Roman engineering. When it passes along a slope its downhill side is made of unusually large kerbstones. It always takes the easiest ground, often deviating some distance from the Wall to do so.

There were 16 forts along the Wall. They all had a characteristic playing-card shape with rounded corners. Most of them were arranged to straddle the Wall, so that one third of the

A model of the fort at Benwell.

fort together with three of its main gateways projected north
of the Wall. This design shows that the intention of placing the
forts on the Wall was not that the garrison could fight from
within the fort, but rather that troops could rapidly issue out
through the main gates and deploy against the enemy in the
open country. There was no regular pattern of spacing, and
intervals between forts varied from three to nine miles. The
size of forts also varied between 3½ acres to 5½ acres. The
smaller forts housed 500 infantry, while the larger ones could
accommodate 500 cavalry or 1000 infantry.

All the forts were built to a similar plan. They were
surrounded by a ditch and defended by a wall about five
feet thick, with an earth rampart piled up against its inner
face. There were at least four gateways, and six if the fort
projected north of the Wall. At the centre of the fort stood
the headquarters building (principia). This had a forecourt
surrounded by colonnades, which gave access to a covered hall
(basilica), and a series of small rooms, the central one being
the regimental chapel. This room contained the regimental
standards and the image of the reigning emperor. In some
forts, most notably at Chesters, it also contained the entrance
to an underground strong-room which held the pay and savings
of the regiment.

On one side of the principia stood the commanding officer's
house (praetorium). This was a court-yard type of house, often

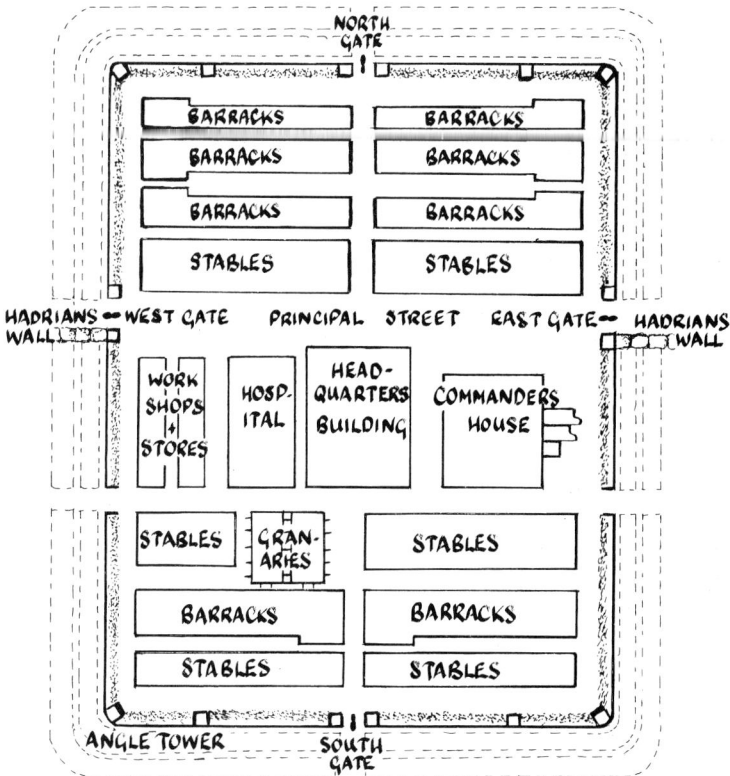

A plan of a typical cavalry fort on Hadrian's Wall.

provided with a private suite of baths. On the other side of the principia were the granaries (horrea). These were massive buttressed buildings with a raised floor to prevent damp. They were designed to hold the grain and other food supplies of the regiment, including a year's reserve supply in case of emergencies. On either side of this central range of buildings were rows of long narrow buildings which contained the barracks for the troops. There were also stables, storehouses and workshops. If the garrison consisted of an infantry regiment, each barrack block housed a century (which actually consisted of 80 men) together with its centurion. If it was a cavalry unit, the block housed two squadrons (turmae)

Barrack blocks at Chesters.

of 32 men, each commanded by a decurion. Whether infantry or cavalry the men were grouped in mess-units of eight, each with their own room for living and sleeping, with an ante-room for kit.

Some forts also had a hospital, a courtyard building surrounded by individual rooms separated by a small passageway. Outside the fort there was usually a bath-house with a suite of rooms graded in temperature from cold to hot. A civilian settlement (vicus) also sprang up outside most forts. Traders were attracted by the presence of the soldiers with their regular incomes and provided the usual range of facilities enjoyed by soldiers in their off-duty hours. Veteran soldiers on completion of their military service would often retire to the settlement outside their former fort. Examples of the shops and taverns to be found in such settlements can be seen at Housesteads and Vindolanda.

There are several ancient sources that tell us the names of the forts along the Wall and of the regiments which formed their garrisons. A document known as the *Notitia Dignitatum*, which dates from the early fifth century but is derived from

The Rudge Cup.

earlier sources, records the distribution of imperial officials throughout the Roman world. It has a section entitled '*Also along the line of the Wall*' listing the regiments and names of 12 of the Wall forts. The ancient names for Carlisle, Corbridge and a few other places near the Wall are given in the *Antonine Itinerary*. This is a handbook on the road system of the Roman empire, produced in the fourth century but using earlier material; this gives place names along various routes together with intervening distances.

The names of five forts at the western end of the Wall are given on the *Rudge Cup*, a small enamelled cup found in a well at Rudge in Wiltshire; this has a decorated frieze showing the Wall with its turrets and milecastles. It is now on display at Alnwick Castle, the home of the Duke of Northumberland. A similar cup found at Amiens in 1949 lists six forts at the western end of the Wall. The sixth century *Ravenna List*, a road map showing the countries, towns and rivers of the known world, also gives the names of forts along the Wall.

In the course of its route from Wallsend to Bowness the Wall had to cross three river valleys, those of the North Tyne, the Irthing and the Eden. Bridges were built at each of these crossings and substantial remains may still be seen at Chesters on the North Tyne and at Willowford on the Irthing. It seems

A legionary soldier (left) and an auxiliary soldier (right) as portrayed by members of the Ermine Street Guard.

that at first these bridges only carried the Wall across but were later enlarged to carry the Military Way as well.

In the west the wall ended at Bowness-on-Solway but the system of frontier control was continued down the coast for 40 miles as far as St Bees. This frontier system consisted of milefortlets built of timber and turf with two stone towers between each pair, just as on the Wall. Troops were housed in forts along the coast.

Hadrian's Wall was never regarded as an independent system standing on its own. A major network of roads and forts led south to the legionary fortresses at York and Chester. There were also forts north of the Wall, whose garrisons were able to deal with minor disturbances and to relay information to the Wall garrison. For most of the time that the Wall was occupied, forts were maintained at Birrens, Netherby and Bewcastle in the western sector, and Risingham and High Rochester in the centre. Each of these forts was strongly garrisoned by a part-mounted regiment 1000 strong allowing a wide zone beyond the Wall to be controlled. The Romans were thus able to gain early warning of any trouble that was brewing and to anticipate any enemy action.

The Roman army consisted of two groups of troops, the legions and the auxiliaries. The legions were the crack troops. Each legion had just over 5000 highly trained and heavily armed infantry together with a small contingent of cavalry. The commander of a legion was a man of senatorial rank appointed by the emperor. The legion was divided into 60 centuries of 80 men, each commanded by a centurion. Legions were recruited exclusively from Roman citizens and included highly skilled craftsmen in their ranks. From the time of Hadrian there were three legions in Britain. The Second Augusta stationed at Caerleon, the Sixth Victrix at York, and the Twentieth Valeria Victrix at Chester. Detachments from all three legions took part in the building of Hadrian's Wall. Each legion was allotted a specified length in which to construct the milecastles, turrets and the Wall as well as digging the Ditch. They worked in labour gangs based on the centuries and recorded their progress by centurial stones, many of which have survived.

The auxiliaries were recruited from non-Roman provincial tribes. They provided the light-armed infantry and most of the cavalry of the Roman army. They were paid less than the legionary soldiers, but on discharge were granted Roman citizenship. They formed smaller units than the legions and were grouped into regiments of either 1000 or 500 strong. These regiments were either infantry or cavalry or some combination of the two. Each infantry regiment was divided into centuries of 80 men commanded by a centurion, while cavalry regiments were divided into squadrons of 32 men under a decurion. The commanding officer of the larger infantry regiments was a tribune, while the commander of the smaller regiments and of all cavalry units was a prefect. The auxiliaries formed the garrison of the Wall frontier and we know the names of many of the units at the various forts.

Hadrian's Wall marked the northern frontier not only of Britain but of the whole Roman empire. Although left abandoned for hundreds of years, robbed of its stone from the medieval period onwards, and engulfed by the remorseless inroads of industry and commerce, it still survives in the central sector as a magnificent memorial to the tenacity and determination of those who built it. The sight of the Wall rising and falling over the high crags of the Whin Sill and dominating the remote and lonely countryside is one of the most impressive in Britain. The outstanding significance of Hadrian's Wall has recently been recognised by its inclusion as a World Heritage site and its wild and lonely setting is attracting an ever growing number of visitors. It is the aim of this book to provide the visitor with a guide to the visible remains and to explain the significance of this important part of our heritage.

# CHAPTER 2

## Wallsend to Newcastle

Wallsend — the name says it all, for the fort at Wallsend marks the eastern extremity of Hadrian's Wall. For the Wall pilgrim it is in fact the beginning, the beginning of an attempt to trace the remains of the most famous barrier in Europe's long history. The name Wallsend also conjures up a different picture of the past, for the town is proud of its share in Britain's industrial history. At one time it was famed for its glass making. For many years it was also a centre of the British coal industry. This provided much needed employment but also brought its share of tragedy, culminating in a terrible accident in June 1835 in which 102 miners, many of them young boys, were lost in a mining explosion. The name of the town was also spread world-wide through its shipyards, especially the Swan Hunter yard which adjoins the Roman fort and is still active today. Here in 1906 the liner *Mauretania* was launched, commissioned by Cunard in an effort to win back from the Germans the Blue Riband for the fastest crossing of the Atlantic. Mauretania achieved this feat in 1909 and retained the title for the next 22 years. She dominated the Atlantic run throughout this period, making the crossing with remarkable speed and regularity. In 1935 on her last voyage to the breaker's yard at Rosyth, she paused off the mouth of the Tyne in a final tribute to the men of Wallsend who had enabled her to become a legend in shipping.

The placing of a fort at Wallsend was not in the original plan for the new frontier established by Hadrian. At first it was intended that the Wall should run westwards from Newcastle, and this was where construction started in AD 122. But it was soon discovered that the Tyne could be forded for some miles to the east of Newcastle, and the decision was taken to extend the Wall eastwards for four miles and to build a fort at Wallsend in order to prevent illicit crossings of the river.

The fort was placed on a raised bank of clay at a bend of the river commanding a clear view both southwards along the

The *Mauretania* leaves the Tyne for her maiden voyage, 1906.

Bill Reach to Bill Quay, and eastwards along the Long Reach to Northumberland Point. The site was chosen to enable the garrison to keep a watchful eye along a five mile stretch of river. The fort's name was Segedunum, which is said to be the Celtic for either 'Strong Fort' or 'Victory Fort'. It occupied an area of just over four acres, had four double gateways and was surrounded by a ditch. Its first garrison was the Second Cohort of Nervians, a 500 strong infantry regiment from Gaul. At some time during the third century this garrison was replaced by another Gallic regiment, the Fourth Cohort of Lingones, who were originally recruited from the south of France.

After the end of Roman rule the fort seems to have been abandoned. Stone was robbed from the site to build the Saxon priories at Jarrow and Tynemouth, and when the antiquarian John Horsley came here in 1772 the fort area had been ploughed over, although the outline of the ramparts could still be traced. In 1781 a coal shaft was sunk near the western rampart and by the early nineteenth century the whole area had become a busy pit village. In 1880 the local community had the opportunity to buy the fort site for £680 but were unable to raise the money, and the area was then covered by housing.

18

In 1929 a number of small excavations were undertaken in order to determine the plan of the fort. In the course of these investigations the archaeologist F. G. Simpson organised a team of retired miners to dig a tunnel under Buddle Street and found that the Wall which ran up to the west gate was of Narrow gauge and was built at the same time as the fort. This showed that both Wall and fort belonged to the second phase of Wall construction and were an afterthought to the original plan. It was not until 1975, however, when the area was being redeveloped, that the whole of the fort site was again opened out for investigation. Excavations continued until 1984 and resulted in the most extensive study of any fort on the Wall.

My first visit here was in 1978 on a day of driving rain with thick mist hanging over the river. The dim silhouette of a line of cranes looming out of the gloom gave the only indication of the nearby Swan Hunter shipyard. A sea of mud, criss-crossed by the remains of demolished tenement houses, marked the site of the fort. It was a dismal sight, and yet the remains of its gritty and sometimes tragic industrial past seemed to represent a genuine picture of Wallsend.

Sadly, the modern redevelopment which has taken place has obscured this industrial heritage and left the area beside the river rather featureless. Go to the site now and you will find that most of the fort area is under grass and the layout of the walls and gateways is marked out in concrete. It is all very neat and tidy, but one is left with the feeling that everything has been sanitised. There is no life here now. Even the archaeologists have gone. What is left is entirely flat and at ground level. So much so that you can park your car ten yards away and not know that you are beside the site of a famous fort.

It seems a pity that the extremities of the fort have not been marked out by low walls, say a foot high, so that one could look across the site and take in its dimensions at a glance. Wallsend today, despite its great significance in the history of the Wall frontier, is sadly lacking in atmosphere and the eager traveller about to set out on a pilgrimage along the Wall will find it a disappointment. Plans have recently been announced to build a section of Wall to its full height on its original line near the west gate of the fort. If these plans come to fruition Wallsend may yet become a worthwhile site to visit.

About one third of the fort lies on the northern side of Buddle Street and site notices indicate the important features. Towards the end of the 18th century a large house known as Carville House was built on the site of the east gate. Stones from the foundation of the gate tower were discovered in 1912 when Carville House was demolished and replaced by a working men's hostel euphemistically called Simpson's Hotel. These stones are now laid out in their original position in the gateway.

A fragment of Wall running for some yards down towards the river is now visible at the south-east corner of the fort. In the early 19th century John Buddle, the manager of the Wallsend Colliery whose father had a house built within the area of the fort, told the famous Wall scholar Dr Collingwood Bruce that he had often seen a stretch of Wall as a boy, when running down from the fort to bathe in the river. In subsequent years all traces of this length of Wall disappeared until it was revealed again in 1903, when Swan Hunter were extending their shipyard for the building of the *Mauretania*. It seems that the purpose of this extra stretch of Wall was to prevent raiders infiltrating between the fort and the river.

The only other original portion of the fort to be seen today is the headquarters building, which lies in a fenced-off sunken area. The central courtyard lies under grass but the stone remains of the regimental offices may be seen. The central room, which has a sunken strong room reached by a flight of stone steps, should be compared with similar rooms at Chesters and Vindolanda. After excavation all the rest of the fort was covered with topsoil and turfed over.

Before leaving the site one should visit the Wallsend Heritage Centre, which adjoins the fort and has interesting displays illustrating both the Roman period and also the town's later industrial history. A mural outside the Centre depicts the history of Wallsend from Roman times through to its later industrial period. Sadly, shortage of staff has meant that the Centre is not regularly open and, when it is, not all the displays are on view.

Any visitor wishing to appreciate fully the significance of the fort at Wallsend and its role in the Roman control of the Tyne should visit the mouth of the river at Tynemouth.

Those travelling by the Metro will arrive at the remarkable Tynemouth station. This was built in 1882 to a design by the North Eastern Railway's chief architect, William Bell, and was admired by thousands of Victorian seaside trippers. Saved from partial demolition in the 1070s, it is now being fully restored. It is notable for the intricate cast iron work which supports a glass roof and is a fine example of Victorian elegance.

Tynemouth stands at the point where the River Tyne flows out into the North Sea. Dominant on the cliffs above the estuary stand the magnificent remains of the Castle and Priory. The original Priory, which stood on the site of an earlier Anglo-Saxon monastery, was destroyed by the Danes in 865 and the Castle was built in 1095. The surviving ruins date from the 11th and 14th centuries. Three kings were buried on the site, Oswin king of Deria in 651, Osired, king of Nórthunbria in 792, and Malcolm III king of Scotland in 1093. They are commemorated by the three crowns which adorn the Borough of North Tyneside coat of arms.

Immediately below the headland on which the Priory stands is the North Pier which runs for three quarters of a mile out to sea. To get a good blow, one should walk its full length. From the end of the pier one has an excellent view of South Shields and can appreciate why the Romans built a fort there to guard the approaches to the river.

Before leaving Tynemouth one should visit the Watch House Museum. This is the headquarters of the Volunteer Life Brigade which was established in 1864 to assist in the shore rescue of the crews of ships in distress. It was the first such body to be established in the United Kingdom. The Museum, which is open every day except Mondays, has a fascinating collection of relics from its long history, including some superb figureheads from former sailing vessels. From its searchlight room there is an excellent view of the river in every direction, including the treacherous Black Midden rocks which present such a hazard to shipping. Admission is free but contributions are welcomed for Brigade funds.

There is an excellent riverside walk linking Tynemouth with North Shields. This passes under the massive monument to Admiral Lord Collingwood, Nelson's second in command at the Battle of Trafalgar, who on board the Royal Sovereign led the

View westwards up the River Tyne from the Collingwood monument, Tynemouth.

British fleet into action on 21 October 1805. The monument is set on a huge rectangular plinth on high ground overlooking the river, and is surrounded by four 30 pounder guns from the Royal Sovereign.

North Shields is the base of the Tyne fishing fleet and famous for its Fish Quay which is a centre of bustling activity. All around are wharves and warehouses, a chandlery, ship's stores, and the whole complex of a fish market. There is also a hostel run by the Royal National Mission to Deep Sea Fishermen whose restaurant is open to the public. The riverside area is currently being developed to create a fishermen's working area, a public walkway and a car-park. Beside the quay are the High and Low Lights, distinctive white towers which date from the beginning of the nineteenth century and were used by approaching vessels to obtain a sight line and avoid the treacherous hidden rocks at the mouth of the river. On the hillside facing the river there is a huge symbol of a fish laid out in concrete. The town of North Shields lies high up on the hill and may be approached from the riverside in several places by steep flights of steps.

Before returning to Wallsend one should cross the river to visit the Roman fort at South Shields. Although not an integral part of the Wall system, this fort made an important contribution to the security of the frontier. From North Shields there is a ferry across the river every thirty minutes, and any waiting time may happily be spent in Ye Old Anchor Teashop, which is strategically placed beside the ferry landing-place.

The Roman fort at South Shields is situated on high ground above the river and commanded an excellent view both eastwards to the river mouth and southwards down Shields Reach. Its Roman name was Arbeia. The history of the site is complicated and much remains unknown. When originally built, it covered an area of just over four acres and probably accommodated a regiment of 480 foot soldiers and some 120 cavalry. Early in the third century it seems to have been used as a supply base for the Roman campaigns in Scotland. Most of the internal buildings were destroyed, 22 granaries were built and the fort was extended southwards. The regiment garrisoning the fort at that time was the Fifth Cohort of Gauls. At the end of the third century the interior of the fort was replanned and barrack buildings were erected on the site of some of the granaries. By the beginning of the fourth century the garrison of Arbeia is known to have consisted of bargemen from the River Tigris in what is now Iraq. They may have been employed ferrying supplies by boat upriver to the forts at Wallsend and Newcastle.

The most striking feature of the fort today is its reconstructed west gate. This is a most impressive structure which dominates the eye from all directions. It is a remarkable construction, built on the foundations of the Roman gate and rising to the full height of the original gateway. The work was undertaken in 1986 by John Laing Construction and was completed in six months by a team of ten men. Great care has been taken to make the reconstruction resemble the original as closely as possible. The same type of sandstone has been used, short lengths of the fort-wall and earth-rampart have been built on either side, and defensive ditches have been dug in front of the gate.

Inside the gateway there are various displays illustrating the life of the fort. In a ground floor room there is a

The reconstructed west gate at South Shields.

quartermaster's store. The quartermaster is seen counting out carrots, and in the corner of the room a cat is about to leap on a mouse which is eating some corn. Sacks of various foods, each with their Latin label, are arranged on the shelves above. Wooden stairs take one up to the first floor, which is level with the wall walkway. Here there is a very fine model of the fort showing its reconstruction as a supply base in the early third century. A second flight of stairs beings one to the top level of the gate. The view from here is magnificent and shows how the fort dominated the river mouth. A plan indicates the main landmarks, including the fort at Wallsend. One can readily understand how through these two forts the Romans could maintain a close watch on the entire length of river from several miles west of Wallsend right down to the river mouth.

In a room on the right there is a group of five soldiers, representing the auxiliary soldiers of the Roman army who would have garrisoned the fort in the mid-second century. A centurion stands in the centre resplendent in decorative bronze mail and kilted leather straps, while to his left there

Auxiliary soldiers at South Shields. They represent (from left to right) a centurion, a standard-bearer and two ordinary soldiers, one of whom is off-duty and munching an apple.

is a standard-bearer with a bearskin cape over his tunic. Two ordinary auxiliary soldiers are seen on the right. The first is on duty and wears an iron mail shirt and iron helmet and carries a short sword. The second has taken off his armour after finishing his tour of duty and is wearing a fine tunic and a large cloak and is happily munching an apple. Sitting in the window on the left is another soldier armed with a bow.

This reconstruction has been meticulously thought out and adds wonderfully to the atmosphere of the fort. Purists may differ over the desirability of building replicas, and in order to build this gateway the planners had to appeal to the Secretary of State who eventually overruled his senior civil servants. Those who visit it today have no doubt that he was right to do so. Not only does one get a realistic impression of the double gateway of a fort, but also excellent use has been made of the various rooms in the structure to provide displays. The fine view of the mouth of the river from the top of the gateway adds to our understanding of the siting of the fort, for the river is not visible today from ground level. The whole impression of this reconstruction seems just right, and there is nothing dead or lifeless about it.

There are several features to be seen in the central area of the fort. The third century headquarters building was constructed around AD 220 and one may pick out the sunken strong room. Part of the commanding officer's house and the outlines of nine granaries are also visible. At the south-eastern corner of the fort the remains of a latrine can be seen built against the earth rampart of the fort wall. Other visible remains include some sections of the fort wall, the north and south gates and the north west and south west angle towers.

The site was first examined in 1875 and it was excavated again in 1949 under Sir Ian Richmond. Since 1983 an extensive programme of investigation has been conducted by Tyne and Wear Museums Service and at the time of writing excavations are in progress in the northern area of the fort and may be watched from a viewing platform.

There is a fine museum on the site. One room is devoted to the life of the Roman soldier and another has exhibits on religion and the rites of death, with examples of cremation and burial. Two very fine tombstones found in the cemetery south of the fort are displayed here. One is of a freedman called Victor who is pictured receiving a cup of wine in paradise. The other was set up by a man called Barates, who came from Palmyra in the Syrian desert, to Regina, a woman who had once been his slave but whom he had later freed and married. She is portrayed sitting in a high-backed wicker chair, with a distaff in her hand and a trinket box and work box with balls of wool beside her. The inscription on the tombstone is uniquely written in two languages, Latin and the language of Palmyra.

There is a small shop where one may buy literature about the site. One should certainly buy the children's guide and go round the fort in the company of young Alba, a dumpy, little, dark-haired boy in goat-skin boots, whose father was the chief standard bearer of the Gallic unit which formed the garrison. There is a further taste of Roman life if you buy the latest copy of the *Arbeia Herald* or decide to join the Cohors Quinta Gallorum! There is considerable information available for school parties, who may even apply to participate in the excavation programme.

Arbeia is an interesting and important site, deservedly popular with visitors. Amazingly there is no charge for admission, either to the fort or to the museum, although there is a moral obligation on all visitors to pay at least the suggested voluntary donation of 25p when they pick up the fort guide. Dominated by its impressive west gate and bustling with the activity which accompanies an excavation, there is a feeling of life and vitality here which is sadly missing at Wallsend.

The pilgrim who is to walk the Wall, however, must now recross the river and return to Wallsend for the journey westwards. The Wall leaves the fort at Wallsend from the southern entrance of the west gate. For the pilgrim about to set out on the long march to Bowness the moment of departure is symbolic. But any feelings of emotion or excitement are short-lived, for between Wallsend and Newcastle modern development has removed all traces of the Wall, and even the landmarks referred to in the latest edition of Collingwood Bruce's *Handbook to the Roman Wall* have in the last few years mostly disappeared.

Those using their cars to explore the Wall should make no delay in heading for the riverside at Newcastle, for they will miss nothing on the way. Walkers have a purgatorial experience in front of them. The four miles between Wallsend and Newcastle have long been an urban sprawl abandoned to the insatiable demands of the motor car. The only compensation is that the line of route is clear: A187 Fossway and up Byker Hill, then along Shields Road, under the Metro bridge and downhill across the Ouse Burn, along New Bridge Street, left down Gibson street, right along City Road, and down to Quayside and the Tyne Bridge.

Those who refer diligently to the Wall *Handbook* will take a little comfort from knowing that on the west side of George Street two altars dedicated to Jupiter Optimus Maximus were found in 1892–3, or that where Fossway crosses Coutts Road is the presumed site of Turret 1b. On the climb up Byker Hill it is rather disconcerting to read that in 1725 the noted antiquarian, William Stukely, here found the Wall to be standing in good order. The only reminder of the Wall in this urban desert

Bridges over the River Tyne at Newcastle. In the foreground is Robert Stephenson's High Level Bridge opened in 1849. Immediately to the east is the dumpy Swing Bridge of 1876, which occupies the site of the Roman bridge. In the background, overtopped by a high arch of girders, is the Tyne Bridge of 1928.

that I could see is the Foss Inn on the approach to the Byker roundabout. This is said to be on the site of Milecastle 2, although even that is disputed; the inn sign which shows the Wall, the Ditch and the Vallum is probably incorrect, since the Vallum is not thought to have been constructed east of Newcastle.

After the hassle of the journey from Wallsend it is a relief to linger awhile on the quayside at Newcastle, which is an attractive and relatively quiet area. On a sunny day it is pleasant to sit out on the riverside terrace beside the Quayside Inn, where one can have a reasonably priced lunch of broth and hobbit, a local name for a filled sandwich. The inn itself is an interesting old building, the only medieval house and warehouse complex with a private quay to survive in Newcastle, and in the last few years it has been pleasingly restored. Nearby is the old fish market, now converted into attractive offices.

The most striking feature seen from the quayside is the close cluster of bridges over the river, illustrating the importance of Newcastle as a communications centre. For the Wall pilgrim the one to note is the attractive, dumpy, little Swing Bridge, which lies on the site of its Roman predecessor, built about AD 120 to carry the road from the south to the new fort of Pons Aelius. Many Roman coins have been found in the river here, thrown from the bridge as offerings to the river-god. Two matching altars, appropriately dedicated to Oceanus and to Neptune and obviously from a shrine on the bridge, were found in the bed of the river, one in 1875 and the other in 1903. Their dedication shows that the shrine was set up by the Sixth Legion and was intended to protect the bridge against flooding. Both may now be seen at the Museum of Antiquities in the University precinct.

The Roman bridge remained in use for over a thousand years, and its piers were used to support its replacement constructed in 1248. This bridge survived until the great flood which engulfed the Tyne in 1771. In 1775 a new bridge was built, which also used the surviving Roman piers, but it was very low and prevented the passage of large ships up river. The present swing bridge was built by Lord Armstrong between 1866 and 1876. It was one of the first large opening bridges in the world.

To the east of the Swing Bridge, overtopped by a high arch of girders is the Tyne Bridge, built in 1928. It is now the main approach to the city from the south. Immediately to the west is the remarkable High Level Bridge constructed by Robert Stephenson and opened in 1849. It is double tiered with the railway running above the road. Its six cast iron arches are supported on stone piers which, in order to reduce weight, are hollow above the high water mark. The three bridges further upstream are the Queen Elizabeth II Bridge which carries the Metro across the river to Gateshead, the King Edward Bridge which takes the main railway line into Newcastle Central Station, and the Redheugh Bridge which carries the A69 across the river.

The fort at Newcastle was called Pons Aelius, taking its name from the bridge built by Hadrian whose family name was Aelius. The exact site of the fort is not known but recent excavations have shown that it lay in the vicinity of the Castle. Remains of the headquarters building and commanding officer's house have been found beside the Keep.

Newcastle is an interesting and attractive city and the visitor should take time to explore its many delights. The centre of the city was laid out by Richard Grainger and John Dobson between 1835 and 1840. Their masterpiece was the gracious Grey Street which sweeps uphill past the stately Theatre Royal to the monument which commemorates Earl Grey of 1832 Reform Act fame. Portions of the medieval city wall survive in the west and one should visit the castle and St Nicholas' Cathedral. Near the river there is a fine cluster of ancient buildings including the historic Guildhall and the fine medieval Bessie Surtees' House. The Laing Art Gallery contains several watercolours by members of the Richardson family which depict the Roman Wall and the forts at Wallsend and Chesters as they were in the middle of the last century. Newcastle also has a proud industrial past. The first steam turbine was made in the city, the light bulb was invented here, and the city is famous for its bottled beer.

For the Wall enthusiast the most important place to visit is the Museum of Antiquities which is sited in the University precinct and contains a most valuable collection of finds associated with the Roman frontier. An outstanding feature of the museum is the fine collection of models made by Mr William Bulmer, a former curator. There are models of milecastles, turrets, a military bath house, a Vallum crossing, the fort at Benwell, and most impressive of all a huge model of the whole length of Hadrian's Wall showing all its associated features. Some of the most famous finds on the Wall are displayed here, including the head of the statue of the Celtic god Antenociticus from his temple at Benwell, a fine sestertius (brass coin) of Hadrian found in the Tyne, and several statues and altars associated with Mithraism, taken from the Mithraic temples at Carrawburgh and Housesteads. A small payment activates the reconstruction of the Mithraic Temple at Carrawburgh. Lights come on and the viewer is treated to an address by a Roman officer who explains the religion of Mithras and its attraction to soldiers. There are life-sized models of a legionary soldier, and an auxiliary cavalryman. There is also a model of an archer,

A reconstruction of the temple of Mithras at Carrawburgh.

based on a tombstone found at Housesteads. No Wall pilgrim should pass through Newcastle without seeing the collection displayed at this museum.

CHAPTER 3

# Newcastle to Portgate

The whole Wall system seems to have been planned to start from the Tyne bridge, since the known milecastle sites to the west of Newcastle were spaced at exact intervals from the river. To follow the line of the Wall one should head north to cross Sandhill and ascend the Castle Stairs to reach the Keep. The steep climb reminds one of the high platform, providing excellent views along the river, on which the Romans placed their fort. The Castle was founded in 1088 by Robert Curthose, the eldest son of William the Conqueror and the Keep was built by Henry II in 1178. From the top of the Keep there is a fine panoramic view of the city. A few Roman remains are displayed in a small museum and information about the fort is given in the Great Hall. The centre of the fort lay close to the north-west corner of the Keep and the outlines of some of the buildings are marked out in the modern paved surface. One should pass left of the Keep and under the railway bridge to emerge into St Nicholas Street beside the Black Gate, which was built 1247–50 as the principal gateway to the castle.

The line of the Wall runs straight ahead westwards, but before continuing the journey one should first visit St Nicholas' Cathedral. Although the Diocese of Newcastle was only founded in 1882, the Cathedral Church of St Nicholas dates almost entirely from the 14th and 15th centuries and is famous for its outstanding lantern tower. There are several fine monuments to distinguished local people. These include Admiral Lord Collingwood, the hero of Trafalgar: Lord Stamfordham, private secretary to Queen Victoria and King George V: Viscount Grey of Fallodon, foreign secretary from 1905 to 1916. A tablet in the south aisle commemorates Captain John Bover RN who died in 1782. He is said to have 'filled with the highest credit the arduous situation of regulating officer of this port'. In fact he was the local pressgang captain and was much feared. A local song refers to sailors who dare not come ashore 'for Bover and his gang'.

All Wall pilgrims should find time to admire the fine marble monument to Dr John Collingwood Bruce (1805–1892), the author of the Wall *Handbook* and the pioneer of modern studies on the Wall. They will also be interested to see, displayed in a glass cabinet on the south wall, a portion of one of the wooden supports of the original Roman bridge over the Tyne. Westgate Road marks the line of the Wall and there is no problem of route finding for the walker. Car drivers will discover that there is a short section of one-way traffic which compels them to turn left out of Westgate Road; they should turn right at the first opportunity, following signs to the General Hospital. The impressive building at the junction with Collingwood Road is the headquarters of the Literary and Philosophical Society of Newcastle upon Tyne. A notice on the wall commemorates George Stephenson 1781–1848, and records that in this building he first demonstarated his miners' safety lamp. Wall devotees, however, will be more excited by the notice on the Miners' Institute next door which reads: 'In this plot covered by red concrete stand the lower courses of the south face of Hadrian's Wall, built first in AD 122 from Newcastle upon Tyne to Bowness on Solway and afterwards extended to Wallsend, a distance in all of 80 Roman miles.' All traces of red concrete have long since disappeared but this is the first official intimation of Hadrian's Wall on the ground since leaving Wallsend. It is a foretaste of the exciting things in store. On the other side of the road there is a statue which impressively bears the one word STEPHENSON.

One should continue along Westgate Road as it inclines north-west away from the station, an impressive building fronted by a fine portico, designed by John Dobson and opened by Queen Victoria in 1850. On the left, an ancient pillar incorporated into a modern building records that this was the former site of the Royal Grammar School, Newcastle, which from 1607 until 1844 occupied the chapel of the 12th century Hospital of St Mary the Virgin.

The Wall is thought to lie under the south side of Westgate Road. At the junction with Bath Lane there is an impressive stretch of the medieval city wall. Westgate Road is very straight and now begins to climb steeply. On reaching the junction with Corporation Street the frustrated pilgrim may take some

The temple of Antenociticus, Benwell.

comfort from knowing that the site of Milecastle 5 was found here and that it is somewhere in this area that there is the furthest point east where the Vallum is credibly recorded. Further solace may be gained from a huge block of high-rise flats on the right called Vallum Court, but since the Vallum lay south of the Wall they would appear to be named without respect for historical accuracy. After passing Newcastle General Hospital one reaches the Church of the Venerable Bede on the corner of Benwell Grove, near which is the supposed site of Milecastle 6.

As one travels westward, Westgate Road becomes West Road, and at the top of a hill lies the site of Benwell, the first fort to the west of Newcastle. Its Roman name was Condercum which means 'The Place with the fine Outlook'. The fort occupied a magnificent site on a high plateau with excellent views in every direction, and was well suited to its name. It was placed here to guard the valley of Denton Burn which lies immediately to the west. There are no remains visible today, though its presence is indicated by the large Department of Employment building,

Condercum House. The southern area of the fort is covered by
the Denhill Park housing estate, and in 1957 extensions to the
Newcastle and Gateshead Water Company reservoir destroyed
its northern third.

There are two important Roman remains in this area.
Opposite the Rutherford Comprehensive School turn left
into Weidner Road and immediately right and then left into
Broomridge Avenue, following signs to Benwell Roman temple.
On the left a little way down this road an extraordinary sight
meets one's eyes. In a gap between rows of demure, rather
prim-looking suburban houses lie the remains of a Roman
temple. It seems a bit odd to go through the front gate of
the house next door in order to enter the temple — but that's
the way it is, and admission is free. The temple is very small,
measuring only 16 feet by 10 feet internally. It is rectangular
with an apse at its southern end where a statue of the god
once stood. It was probably built late in the second century
AD by the Cohort of Vangiones from Germany, the cavalry
regiment who formed the garrison of Benwell Fort. The altars
that flank the apse are replicas of the originals which are now
in the Museum of Antiquities at Newcastle. The temple was
dedicated to the Celtic god Antenociticus, who was either a local
deity or one whose worship was imported from Germany by the
fort garrison. It is the first surviving piece of Roman masonry
to be seen since leaving Wallsend.

After returning to West Road one should take the next
turning left into Denhill Park. At its southern end lies the
only example of a Vallum crossing to survive from the Wall
system. The Vallum was the earthwork which ran south of
Hadrian's Wall for most of its length and consisted of a ditch
with two mounds on either side of it. The site of the Benwell
Vallum crossing occupies the whole width of the central area
of the housing estate and lies about ten feet below ground
level, surrounded by iron railings. This crossing gave access
to the fort by a causeway across the Vallum. It was faced with
masonry and carried a metalled roadway. A gateway stood
in the centre and a large stone which formed the base of
one side of it can be seen still in position. A reconstruction
drawing of the crossing is depicted on a notice at the far side
of the site. Admission is free, but on my last visit the gate in

The Vallum crossing, Benwell.

the railings was padlocked and there appeared to be no means of gaining entry.

From Benwell fort the road descends to the valley of Denton Burn. After passing a Methodist Church, where in 1953 some traces of the Wall were found in the garden, we come at last to the first fragment of Wall to be seen from the east. This is a stretch about 20 yards long which was purchased by the city of Newcastle in 1924. It lies just in front of Charlie Brown's Auto Centre, fenced in on three sides, and sadly littered with glass. In the Wall *Handbook* there is an engraving showing this stretch of Wall in rustic surroundings as it was in 1848. It is Broad Wall over nine feet thick, showing that it was constructed in the first phase of Wall development. Pause for a while; this is an exciting moment. It is the first trace of the Wall in the seven miles from Wallsend, and there's far more to see further west.

About a third of a mile further on, as one breasts a short rise, there is a second, much finer section of Wall surrounded by grass and set back from the road. This stretch of Broad Wall is about 100 yards in length and contains the well-preserved

The first fragment of Wall at Denton Burn.

Denton Turret (Turret 7b). The turret is recessed five feet into the Wall and its walls rise to six courses in places. Traces of steps survive in the south-west corner. We now have to cross the junction with the newly constructed Western Bypass and the pressure of traffic is redoubled. Just west of the bypass there is a very short section of Wall between the service road, aptly named The Ramparts, and the busy dual carriageway.

At West Denton it is a relief to divert left on to the B6528 to Walbottle. School playing fields on the left provide a foretaste of more open country and one at last has the feeling of leaving Newcastle behind. The road descends to skirt the northern end of Walbottle. At the far end of the village one passes an inn called The Original Masons, although it is not clear whether this is a reference to Roman legionary soldiers. After crossing the wooded Walbottle Dene one enters the village of Throckley, an uninspiring settlement of mainly modern housing, which does, however, boast an excellent fish and chips cafe. Hadrian's Place on the left and Lanercost Gardens on the right remind one of its historical environment and there are excellent views of the Tyne valley to the south.

Denton Turret, with traces of steps in the south-west corner.

An inn on the right of the road has the unusual title of The Royal French Arms and an adjoining row of houses is named Frenchman's Row. These houses were erected in 1796 by the lessees of Heddon Colliery, Messrs Bevin and Brown, to accommodate their miners. But owing to a slump in the coal trade the houses were not required for miners, and from 1796 to 1802 they were the homes of French royalist clergy, who were refugees from the French revolution. The house at the east end of the Row was run as a small tavern by the priests. They received one shilling a day from the British Government until they returned to France after the Peace of Amiens in March 1802. On leaving, the priests erected a sundial with the words 'Time flies, Memory remains', and a Latin inscription thanking the British people for their hospitality. The present public house was built in 1897 and the houses of Frenchman's Row were rebuilt by the Castleward Rural District Council in 1962. The new houses have a sundial but no inscription is visible.

As one approaches Heddon-on-the-Wall traces of the Ditch may be seen on the right of the road, and there are a few signs of the Vallum to the left. Then at the brow of a hill just before entering the village a fine stretch of Wall comes into view in a field on the left. Access is through a gate at its western end. This stretch of Wall is over 100 yards long, built at Broad gauge more than ten feet wide. It rises to seven courses high in some places and the Ditch in front is clearly visible. Near its western end a circular kiln, which is probably medieval, has been built into the thickness of the Wall. Set in a lovely expanse of grassland this stretch of Wall presents a fine sight and is a foretaste of what is in store further west.

Heddon is a quiet little village, in a pleasant setting off the main road. Its street names have a distinctly Roman flavour: Marius Avenue, Antonine Walk, Centurion Way. St Andrew's Church dates back to Anglo-Saxon times and is largely built out of Wall stones. From Heddon there is a half-hourly service to Newcastle and an hourly service to Carlisle, making it an excellent centre from which to explore the wall.

On leaving the village one should bear right on to the B6318, which does a zigzag over the busy A69 and then heads westward towards Harlow Hill. This is the Military Road built by the government in 1751 over the foundations of the Roman Wall. One can now begin to appreciate the various features of the Wall system in relation to one another. There are traces of the Ditch to the north of the road, the road itself is on the line of the Wall, and in several places you can see the Vallum on the left.

After about a mile one passes on the left the farm of Rudchester. This lies just outside the eastern rampart of the Roman fort of Vindobala, the fourth fort along the line of the Wall. The fort covered 4½ acres and lies on a grassy platform astride the road, but there is little to see today. The ground falls sharply both to the east and to the west, showing what a commanding position the fort occupied. In the 4th century its garrison consisted of the First Cohort of Frisians, a 500 strong infantry regiment recruited from an area in what is now Holland.

The road runs in a straight line and can be seen far in the distance climbing up to Harlow Hill. There is no sign of the Wall here but we have the satisfaction of knowing that we are following its line. There are occasional traces of the Vallum to the left, marked out by trees growing on either side, and as we start the long climb up Harlow Hill there are signs of the Ditch to the right, with gorse and hawthorne growing in its banks.

Harlow Hill consists of some half dozen solid, sombre-looking houses on the right of the road, all probably constructed of Wall stones. A pillar box, a telephone kiosk, a chapel and a garage provide its only amenities. When William Hutton stayed at an inn here in 1801 he had an uncomfortable hour or two until his companions realised from his conversation that he was not a spy employed by the government! Early editions of Collingwood Bruce's Wall *Handbook* report that at Harlow Hill 'simple refreshments may be obtained at the temperance hotel, and if need be a bed'. In 1921 the writer, Jessie Mothersole, wrote to the hotel booking a bed, only to receive a postcard with the intriguing reply: 'No temperance at Harlow Hill.' She later discovered that the hotel had been closed during the 1914–18 war. On my last visit a van outside the garage, bearing the name T. Tulip and Sons, Heddon on the Wall, brought back the memory of William Hutton's experience a few miles further west in 1801. Much to his horror he found the servants of the landowner, a Mr Henry Tulip, demolishing the Wall in order to erect a farm house. He begged them to desist, informing them that he had travelled six hundred miles to see it. One can only hope that Mr Tulip's descendants have more respect for what remains of the Wall!

On descending Harlow Hill the road runs straight for over a mile and in several places the Ditch is very clearly defined on the right. A mile west of the Whittledene Reservoir one reaches the little settlement of East Wallhouses. This consists of two or three houses and, surprisingly in this remote setting, a pub, the Robin Hood Inn. My first visit here was on a cold April day of driving rain and bitter wind. I had been walking from Newcastle and reached the inn just after 5 pm. It was Grand National Day and to my surprise the inn was open, and a group of men were playing cards round the fire. I asked for a hot drink and something to eat. The landlord said that although it was a bit early he never turned away anyone who was cold and hungry. He brought me a beef sandwich and a coffee which he said would get me on to Corbridge. I sat in a window seat, with the wind howling round the pub seemingly threatening to tear it down, and felt very grateful.

Halton Tower.

West of the Robin Hood Inn there are distinct traces of the Vallum on the left of the road and one farm, appropriately called Vallum Farm, is actually built over it. The Ditch is also very deep here and in springtime is a pretty sight with primroses, celandines and buttercups growing in its banks.

Two miles to the west of the little hamlet of Halton Shields, the Military Road bisects the fort of Haltonchesters, whose ancient name was Onnum, 'The Rock'. This is $7\frac{1}{2}$ miles west of Rudchester and is the fifth fort on the line of the Wall. The only traces of the fort today are grass mounds beside the gates giving access to the Halton Tower estate. To the west the ground drops steeply to the valley of the Fence Burn, which provided the fort's water supply. When it was first built the fort occupied $4\frac{1}{4}$ acres and was built across the line of the Ditch which had to be obliterated. It was garrisoned by a cavalry regiment, the First Ala of Sabinian Pannonians, a detachment recruited by a certain Sabinus in what is now western Hungary. At some later date the fort was enlarged by an extra half acre, giving it a strange L-shape but the purpose of this enlargement is not known.

One should pass through the gates and follow the public footpath along the road to view Halton Tower. This is a delightful cluster of buildings, whose main feature is a 14th century house built of Roman stones, with a fragment of a 15th century house forming its north wing. Alongside is a Norman chapel which was rebuilt in the early 17th century. A tablet above the pulpit commemorates George Hodgson, a former minister, who had the distinction of being born on Christmas Day 1821 and of dying on Easter Day 1886. One of the tombstones in the churchyard is a large Roman altar placed upside down.

In just under a mile one reaches the important junction of Portgate, where the Wall was crossed by Dere Street, the Roman road linking the Wall with the legionary headquarters of York in the south, and with the outpost forts of Risingham and High Rochester to the north. Dere Street seems to have crossed the Wall through a special guard-house or gateway of which there is no trace today. Portgate now marks the intersection of the Military Road with the busy A68 from Darlington to Jedburgh.

From Portgate one should make an excursion to visit the outpost forts of Risingham and High Rochester. This is a fine journey along the A68, which mainly follows the line of Dere Street, with extensive views of remote and lovely country. Risingham lies 14 miles north of Portgate on the edge of the village of West Woodburn. One should turn left down a farm road immediately after entering the village. The fort, which occupied four acres and was known as Habitancum in Roman times, is seen as a grass covered platform on one's right. One should ask permission at the farm to inspect the ruins. It is possible to do a complete circuit of the ramparts, noting the position of each of the main gates. Some huge blocks of stone lie on the grass outside the west gate and some massive masonry is visible at the rounded north-east angle. The northern rampart has been eroded by the River Rede which has changed its course since Roman times.

The fort of High Rochester is $8\frac{1}{2}$ miles north of Risingham and is approached by a minor road from Rochester village. One should turn right just past a war memorial immediately after entering the village. The porch of the old school-house at the road junction is decorated in an unusual style with Roman stones. After a quarter of a mile the road levels off as it passes through a cluster of houses surrounding a village green. These

The west gate at High Rochester.

houses occupy the central portion of the fort which was just over five acres in size. The huge blocks of an interval tower are clearly visible on the left of the road as one enters the settlement.

One should pass through a gate on the west to view the western rampart and the fine west gate which survives to a considerable height. With a little ingenuity one can do a complete traverse of the ramparts, being careful only to enter fields by their gates. Considerable traces of the rampart wall may be seen lying under grass several courses high. This wall is very thick and is thought to have been designed to support the weight of artillery machines. High Rochester, like Risingham, has yielded a large number of inscribed stones, many of which are in the museum at Newcastle. The ancient name of the fort was Bremenium, The Place of the Roaring Stream, a reference to the site's fine position overlooking the Rede valley. High Rochester is an attractive little settlement and one cannot help contrasting the peaceful scene today with the noise and bustle there must have been in Roman times.

# CHAPTER 4

## *Portgate to Chesters*

Three miles south of Portgate on the outskirts of the village of
Corbridge lies the Roman site of Corstopitum. This occupies
an area of 22 acres and was an important centre in Roman
times. It lay at the strategic point where Dere Street crossed
the Stanegate (the Roman road linking Corbridge with Carlisle)
and for much of its occupation it acted as a supply base for the
army in the north.

A fort was established at Corbridge about AD 85 and the
site remained in military use for about 80 years. In the 160s
AD exclusive military occupation came to an end and shortly
afterwards new granaries, a fountain, temples, shops and a
large courtyard building, were laid out on the site. But this
civilian redevelopment scheme was never fully completed. It
appears to have been halted because of raids by northern
tribes at some time in the late second century. Early in the
third century two compounds of buildings for military use
were laid out south of the main road across the site. These
were used by detachments of the Sixth and Twentieth legions
and were retained in military use until the end of the Roman
period. They contained work shops, store-rooms, housing for
officers and small administrative blocks. It seems that in this
period Corbridge was a garrison town rather like Aldershot or
Catterick. The remains that are visible today form only a small
central part of a much larger town that was one of the major
civilian centres in the northern frontier zone.

The granaries with their massive stone flags and strong
supporting buttresses are particularly impressive. They were
constructed sometime at the end of the second century. They
have a loading platform under a portico which fronts on to the
Stanegate, the east-west road running through the site. Portions
of the flat stone floor can be seen inside, and underneath are
the ventilation ducts which allowed air to circulate.

An aqueduct bringing water into the site from the north fed
a fountain beside the Stanegate and a decorative fountain house

The west granary, Corbridge.

was constructed, which bore a pediment recording that it was built by the Twentieth Legion. The immense amount of wear on the sides of the rectangular water-tank, possibly caused by soldiers sharpening their swords, shows that for a considerable time the tank cannot have held water. Other buildings which may be seen on the site include a huge unfinished courtyard building, the fort headquarters, and some temples at the south-eastern end of the Stanegate.

Corbridge has an excellent museum, housed in a modern, well-lit building. Here one may borrow a taped commentary explaining the most important features of the site. A major exhibit is the famous Corbridge Hoard, the contents of an armourer's workshop which, together with a soldier's breast-plate, were buried beneath a room in the hospital when the first timber fort was destroyed by fire in AD 105. There are some excellent dedication stones, for which both the Latin text and an English translation is provided. A famous piece of sculpture is the Corbridge Lion. This depicts a stag being attacked by a lion. It was found in the cistern of a building which may have been a guest-house. It was probably carved

The underground strong-room, Corbridge.

as a monument for a grave, but later a hole was cut through the lion's mouth and it was reused as a fountain. There is also a life-sized model of a legionary soldier, who is wearing armour copied from the armour in the Corbridge Hoard. A model of the nearby Roman bridge over the Tyne gives one an excellent idea of how the bridge must have looked.

The modern village of Corbridge lies about half a mile from the Roman site. The market place is the ancient centre of the village and it is dominated by St Andrew's Church, portions of which date back to the seventh century, although most of the present building is from the 13th century. It is mainly built of dressed Roman stones obtained from the fort. Inside the church the arch between the tower and the nave is Roman and seems to have been taken in one piece from the site at Corstopitum. The 14th century peel tower in the churchyard is also constructed of Roman stones. It was once a fortified vicarage and is now used as the tourist information office for the town.

In 1122 Henry I visited Corbridge and granted the revenues of the church to the newly founded Priory of Carlisle. This

The Roman arch in St Andrew's Church, Corbridge.

link survives to this day, as the Vicars of Corbridge are still appointed by the Dean and Chapter of Carlisle Cathedral in conjunction with the Bishop of Newcastle. In 1201 King John visited Corbridge and hearing a rumour of buried treasure at Corstopitum set men to work digging there. Their efforts were fruitless but nonetheless Corbridge was granted a town charter. It is fortunate that his diggers did not discover the hoard of 159 gold coins found a foot below the surface in 1911.

The present seven-arched bridge over the Tyne, which replaced an earlier medieval bridge, was completed in 1674 and widened in 1881. It is the only bridge in the whole length of the Tyne to survive the severe flood of 1771, when the water was so high that people could lean over the parapet to wash their hands. The original Roman bridge which carried Dere Street across to the fort of Corstopitum lay further to the west. Its south abutment and the first five piers from the southern end may still be seen when the river is low.

Corbridge was an important centre in the 13th century when its population was about 1500, and its roll of taxpayers contained 77 names, making it the second most important town in Northumberland after Newcastle. But between 1296 and 1350 Corbridge was burned or occupied by Scottish armies six times and the town gradually declined in importance. A survey taken in 1663 showed that its weekly market had been abandoned.

Three miles to the west of Corbridge lies the ancient town of Hexham. Hexham does not seem to have been occupied in Roman times and its known history starts from the seventh century when St Wilfrid chose it for the site of the magnificent abbey which dominates the town today. The abbey church was largely built out of the stones readily available from the nearby site of Corstopitum.

Hexham has suffered much from raiders. In AD 875 the Danes landed and destroyed the abbey church and in 1113 it was refounded as an Augustinian Priory but Scottish raids at the end of the 13th century prevented the completion of the building. In 1297 a band of Scottish raiders herded together a group of schoolboys in the grammar school and after blocking the doors set fire to the building. Hexham never recovered from these raids, although the abbey church has been beautifully restored and the nave was completed in 1908.

There are some fine things to see in the Abbey. The frith-stool or bishop's seat, later used as a seat of sanctuary assuring its occupant of safety, is the only surviving piece of furniture from Wilfrid's original church. The night stairway with its 35 steps leading to the dormitory of the canons is a prominent feature of the Abbey and conjures up the picture of cowled monks ascending to their dormitory, which is now used as a robing room by the abbey choir. There is a fine Roman tombstone depicting a mounted soldier riding over the prostrate figure of a barbarian. This is the grave stone of Flavinus, the standard bearer of a cavalry regiment who died at the age of 25 and was buried at Corstopitum. Another striking feature of the Abbey is the Saxon crypt reached by a stairway from the central aisle of the nave. This is built out of Roman stones. One stone which has been reused in the roof bears an inscription with the names of Severus, the emperor who died at York in AD 211, and his two sons, Geta and Caracalla. The name of the younger son Geta was erased after his murder by his brother in AD 212. The eighth century cross of Bishop Acca and the Saxon font are also notable features.

Hexham today is a busy but attractive country town. It was granted a market in 1239 by Henry III. The oldest purpose-built prison in England, now known as the Manor Office, is to be found here. This was built on the orders of Archbishop Melton of York in 1330 and is constructed almost entirely of Roman stones taken from Corstopitum. Another impressive building is the Moot Hall. This was built about 1400 as a gateway and was used as a courthouse until 1838. It is unfortunate that the environment of such an historic and pleasant town has now been disfigured by a large industrial complex situated to the east. This obviously provides much needed employment for local people, but no attempt appears to have been made to fit it into the landscape or to conceal its particularly hideous appearance.

From Hexham one should return to Portgate and continue westwards along the line of the Wall. The road climbs steadily for a couple of miles, passing through attractive open country giving fine views in almost all directions. On the left there are

The Ditch west of Portgate.

many traces of the gorse-covered banks of the Vallum, while to the north the Ditch can be picked out for a long way ahead. To obtain relief from incessant road-walking it is possible to walk for some way along the south mound of the Ditch, but frequent field walls block the path, forcing one continually to rejoin the road. It would seem a good idea if a path was created along these stretches of Ditch. They lie in a strip of land which is of no use for farming and could easily be linked by stiles over the crosswalls.

At the roadside just after passing St Oswald's Hill Head Farm there is a simple wooden cross about 12 feet high beside a notice recording the battle of Heavenfield which took place near this site in AD 635. Oswald, the Christian king of Northumbria, who had been brought up by the monks of Iona, was attacked by the pagan British king, Cadwallon who ruled over North Wales. The two forces met here at a place which has ever since been called Hefenfelth or Heavenfield. On the night before the battle Oswald erected a wooden cross on the high ground where the church now stands and gathered his men to pray for victory. Not much is known about the actual battle, although

The cross at Heavenfield with St Oswald's Church in the background.

it seems that Cadwallon had far superior forces. But the army of Oswald, charged with religious fervour and fighting for the very existence of Northumbria, gained the upper hand and put Cadwallon's forces to rout. They fled in various directions and the discovery of a large number of skulls and sword hilts in a field to the south of the Military Road suggests that at some stage the battle surged over Hadrian's Wall. One of Oswald's first acts after the battle was to invite the monks of Iona to set up a religious house in his kingdom. Under the leadership of Aidan a monastery was founded at Lindisfarne (Holy Island), and from there Christianity spread throughout the whole country. The wooden cross by the roadside was erected by a group of local people in the 1930s to commemorate the battle.

Behind the cross lies the little church of St Oswald. This was rebuilt in 1737 leaving no trace of the original church built by the monks of Hexham on the site where Oswald erected his cross. The church is situated in a field surrounded on three sides by a fringe of trees and is approached by a broad grassy path. It is set back from the road in a quiet and peaceful setting and the visitor senses that this is a holy and ancient place. A notice from the local congregation welcomes visitors to this hallowed spot and expresses the wish that peace may be with them on their journey. This has been a place of pilgrimage from ancient times and for centuries the exact position where Oswald raised the cross was marked by a large stone cross set on top of a Roman altar. This cross has long since disappeared but the altar which was used as its base is now in the church. The simple interior with its pitch-pine benches and white-washed walls enhances the atmosphere of peace. In the east window there are representations of Aidan and Oswald and there is an old sundial built into the south wall which bears the date 1737, the year of the church's construction.

Half a mile further west, shortly after passing Planetrees Farm on the left, we come to the first stretch of Wall since leaving the village of Heddon. This is approached by steps over the field wall opposite the entrance to the Black Pasture Quarry. It was here on 22 July 1801 that William Hutton had his encounter with the local landowner, Mr Henry Tulip. He was horrified to find him engaged in destroying the Wall to build a farm house. According to local tradition it was due to his tears and entreaties that this fine stretch was spared from demolition. This section of Wall is about 30 yards long and four courses high at its highest, and especially interesting in that it preserves a junction of Broad Wall with a narrow section only six feet thick.

The road now descends steeply to the village of Chollerford in the North Tyne valley. There is a very fine section of Ditch on the left and in the grounds of Brunton House there are the remains of what is probably the finest example of any turret on the line of the Wall. This is approached from the Hexham road (A6079), where an English Heritage sign and a stile indicate the route across a gently sloping meadow. On my last two visits there has been a notice saying that the site is temporarily closed because of the dangerous condition of the trees. This notice has now been displayed for some months and most visitors are so anxious to visit this outstanding turret that they ignore the warning and cross the field, cautiously skirting the trees and keeping a wary eye open. I must say that to the untrained eye there appeared to be little cause for concern.

Brunton Turret.

The rear wall of Brunton Turret (Turret 26b) stands 11 courses high and reaches a height of $8\frac{1}{2}$ feet. When the turret was built it was equipped with wing walls of Broad gauge and a stretch of massive Broad Wall between nine and ten feet thick adjoins it to the west. But the Wall which joins the turret to the east, although built on a Broad foundation, is a mere six feet wide. The remains of the Wall and Turret at Brunton are very fine and should on no account be missed. They lie in a beautiful pastoral setting in a meadow which gently slopes towards the river.

Before crossing the river one should visit the remains of the Roman bridge that carried the Wall system over the North Tyne. This lies about half a mile down river. The path to the bridge abutment starts just to the east of the present road bridge and runs along a disused railway line. The massive remains of the bridge abutment are very impressive, and embedded in it there is masonry from a pier of an earlier bridge on the site. This first bridge was erected in the early 120s AD, in the first phase of Wall building. It was built of

The eastern bridge abutment, Chesters.

timber supported on stone piers and was designed to carry the Wall walk-way acros the river.

Early in the third century it was decided to rebuild the bridge in stone on a much larger scale to carry the Military Way, and it is mostly the ruins of this second bridge which are seen today. Abutments stood on each bank, built of large well-dressed sandstone blocks bound together with iron bars. The western abutment now lies in the river. The bridge had three piers which supported four stone arches. Stones recovered from the bed of the river show that the carriageway possessed a parapet decorated at intervals with columns and altars. The architectural and engineering achievement of this bridge was immense and it is one of the most remarkable features on the whole line of the Wall.

The bridge had three piers, the easternmost of which lies under the present east bank of the river. The two other piers can occasionally be seen in the bed of the river when the water is very low. On its northern side there are signs of a channel running across the abutment, which may have been a mill race.

The abutment was built of massive stones which were bound together by iron rods set in lead and the lewis-holes, by which they were lifted into position using iron wedges, can still be seen. At ground level one should note the serrated cutaway of the bridge showing clear indications of being worn by water, and on the northern side there is a phallus symbol, the Roman sign for good luck. Among the stones lying on the site is an impressive pillar which may have been one of a pair decorating the start of the bridge. One should ignore the pile of stones neatly placed beside the river and surrounded by a stone wall. These were put there during the War by German prisoners of war who were brought in to tidy up the site. The Wall running down to the bridge survives to over eight feet in places and is of Narrow gauge built on a Broad foundation. Until recently the western abutment on the other side of the river was not visible, but it is currently being excavated and appears to be of a similar design.

Before crossing the North Tyne one should visit Chollerton Church, which is one and a half miles further up river. The columns of the south side of the nave are re-used Roman pillars, probably taken from the fort at Chesters. The font consists of an inverted Roman altar, which was dedicated to Jupiter Optimus Maximus. A similar font is in use in the church at Haydon Bridge.

Chollerford Bridge which takes the modern road over the North Tyne was built in 1775. Its predecessor, whose piers and abutments may be seen at low water immediately downstream, was destroyed in the floods which swept the Tyne in 1771. Remains of an earlier medieval bridge now lie some 300 yards downstream. To the right lies the extensively enlarged George Hotel. After crossing the river the Military Road turns left to head westwards for Chesters and the open Wall country.

The fort at Chesters lies on a grassy slope above the river and enjoys one of the most attractive settings of any site on the Wall. In Roman times the fort was known by its Celtic name, Cilurnum, meaning 'The Cauldron Pool', probably a reference to the swirling waters of the North Tyne. It was intended to protect the point at which the Wall crossed the river. At the time the fort was constructed parts of the Wall and turret 27a had already been built on the site and had to be demolished.

There is much to see here. Substantial remains of the gates, barracks, headquarters building and commandant's house are exposed to view, and between the fort and the North Tyne stands what is probably the finest military bath house in Britain. Chesters occupies an area of 5¾ acres and about one third of the fort, including its main north, west and east gates, projects north of the Wall. For most of its occupation it housed an auxiliary cavalry regiment 500 strong and from the late second century AD onwards the garrison was provided by the Second Ala of Asturians, recruited originally in north-west Spain.

The major features of the site lie within fenced enclosures. The best order for viewing them is that laid out in the English Heritage guide, which examines the perimeter of the fort and the bath house first, before visiting the central buildings. Notices describe each feature, accompanied by excellent site plans and often by reconstruction drawings. From the entrance a path leads to the north gate where one may start one's visit.

The north gate lies north of the Wall and was originally built as a double gateway protected by twin guardchambers. The central stop-blocks and sockets for both gates can be seen. The western entrance passage was blocked soon after construction, and when the blocking was removed on excavation in the 19th century the earliest levels were seen to be little worn. An aqueduct covered with stone slabs entered the fort at this gate.

The west gate was also a double gateway, opening out north of the Wall, which can here be seen abutting the fort wall near the south gatetower. Comparatively soon after construction, both entrances were blocked. The north guardchamber contains a stone platform for a water tank, fed by an aqueduct which approached the fort from the west. After entering the fort, the water would be channelled off to serve the needs of the garrison for washing, cooking, drainage and sewage disposal. Outside the north guardchamber there is a bakehouse containing an oven for the baking of bread.

The south gate was also originally planned as a double entrance, but, as at the north gate, the passage of the western entrance was blocked soon after construction and only removed on excavation in 1879. The eastern gateway remained in use throughout the Roman period, and one may see that the level of the road has been considerably raised over the period of

The bath house at Chesters, seen from the east bank of the River North Tyne.

occupation. Much of the south wall of the fort may be seen and the south-east angle tower is very well preserved, standing to a height of 11 courses.

The bath house at Chesters is one of the best preserved Roman military bath houses to survive. It had a long and complicated history and English Heritage notices provide an excellent description of the uses of the various rooms at its most developed and extended stage. Bathers entered through a small porch into a communal changing room. In the west wall there are seven prominent niches, which may have been used as cupboards or may have contained statues. It has sometimes been suggested that they were lockers for the bathers' clothing, but there do not seem to have been enough of them to serve this purpose. A doorway at the south-west corner of the room led to a lobby, where the bather could choose between three treatments. On the right he would find hot dry treatment, by going ahead he would enter the warm steam-heat rooms, and by turning left he entered the cold room.

The two hot rooms, which were late additions to the bath

suite, provided hot and dry treatment. The hot dry room was heated by its own separate furnace which burnt charcoal to provide the necessary high temperature. The suite of warm and moist rooms provided treatment similar to a modern sauna. There were three warm rooms, with varying degrees of heat (depending on the distance from the stoke-holes), and a hot room in which the bathers would scrape dirt out of their pores with strigils. In an apsidal room off the hot room was the hot bath. This room was roofed with a barrel vault of tiles and tufa, thus enabling hot air to circulate not only under the floor but through the ceiling as well. The cold room was left unheated, and there was a cold water basin in the centre of the floor. A cold plunge-bath, originally in a separate room to the east, was later inserted in the north-east corner of this room. Towards the river at a lower level than the other rooms there was a latrine, flushed by continuous running water. There would have been wooden seats over the drainage channel on the north and west sides.

At the time of writing excavations by Tyne and Wear Museums Service are in progress on the approach to the western end of the Roman bridge. A notice explains the excavations and displays a painting of the bridge. The current excavations have uncovered part of a ramp and the fortifications of a gatehouse through which the road passed on to the bridge. Traces of the ramp are now clearly visible and once the excavation is complete all the remains uncovered will be laid out for display.

Retracing one's steps one enters the fort by the main east gate which is one of the best preserved on Hadrian's Wall. One should note in particular its southern gateway which survives up to the beginning of the arch. When the gate was excavated in the 19th century it was found that both entrance passageways had been blocked. This blocking was probably inserted soon after the fort's construction, since both of the thresholds are relatively unworn.

In the north-east corner of the fort a pair of barrack blocks may be seen. Each had quarters for the centurion and his deputy at the eastern end, with a series of rooms for the men fronted by a verandah. The two barrack blocks face each other across a street with a central drain and an artist's impression of the scene as it would have been in Roman times is displayed nearby.

The underground strong-room, Chesters.

The headquarters building lay in the central area of the fort. This consisted of two main elements, a courtyard surrounded by a portico or colonnaded walk, and a large hall with a series of small rooms off it. The courtyard had a paved floor and contained a well. On the paving there is a phallic symbol, which in Roman times was used to avert the evil eye and to gain good luck. A painting shows an artist's impression of the view across the courtyard from the north-west corner. The hall was narrow but extended across the whole width of the headquarters building, and had an entrance at both ends. At its western end there was a raised platform (tribunal), where the commanding officer sat on formal or ceremonial occasions.

Beyond the cross-hall lay five rooms which served as the unit's administrative offices. The central room was the regimental chapel, where statues or paintings of the reigning emperor were kept, together with the unit's standards. The rooms on either side were used for regimental records and for accounts. Early in the third century a large underground

Hypocaust pillars in the bath block of the commanding officer's house, Chesters.

strong-room was inserted, which was reached by a flight of steps from the central chapel. An iron-studded oak door was found at the entrance but it fell to pieces shortly after being exposed.

East of the headquarters building lie three blocks of buildings which are very difficult to interpret. The visible remains seem originally to have formed a spacious house for the commanding officer. Several later additions have been made, including the insertion of hypocaust under-floor heating into several of the rooms. At the eastern end lay a bath block with a series of hypocaust floors and tanks.

The museum at Chesters is a very attractive stone building, which was specially designed to house the collection of John Clayton (1792–1890) who owned the Chesters Estate. He was a noted classical scholar and, after excavating the Roman fort of Chesters which lay in front of his house, devoted himself to the systematic exploration of neighbouring forts, milecastles and turrets. As you enter the museum, notice to the left of the doorway a huge rock bearing the inscription PETRA FLAVI

CARANTINI, 'the rock of Flavius Carantinus'. This was inscribed by a Roman soldier of that name when he was quarrying on nearby Fallowfield Fell.

The museum houses a magnificent collection of Roman inscriptions, sculptures and other finds from Chesters and from neighbouring sites, many of them excavated by Clayton himself. It is a lovely period piece. It consists of two rooms, a long hall and a small inner room, and has a delightfully old-fashioned air. One wall of the hall is entirely devoted to inscribed stones. There are five inscribed milestones and a collection of over twenty millstones. There are several finds from the Well of Coventina at Carrawburgh and from the Mithraic temple at Housesteads. There is a good display of iron tools and weapons found at Chesters, and a model of the fort as it might have appeared at the beginning of the third century.

One of the most interesting finds is an official corn measure in bronze which was found by a postman outside the fort of Carvoran in 1915. This holds considerably more than its stated capacity and has sometimes been regarded as a way by which the Roman tax collectors cheated the native British farmers. But it may have had an internal rim to match its stated measure. Another theory is that it was designed to hold a soldier's ration for a week. Probably the most famous find made in the fort was the Chesters Diploma. This was a bronze tablet granting citizenship to an auxiliary soldier on completion of 25 years service. It consisted of two thin bronze plates hinged together to form a four page document. It recorded details of the soldier's service and, in addition to granting him full citizenship, legalised any marriage he might make. The discovery of this document was a unique find in Britain. Clayton presented the original to the British Museum, but an exact replica is on display in the museum here. A significant recent discovery has been a fragment from a gravestone showing a man wearing a Roman toga, a very unusual find in Britain where the toga does not seem to have been normally worn.

Chesters is a delightful site to visit. It is set in attractive parkland on a gentle slope above the river. There is much to see and the remains are very well described. One may also visit Lucullus' Larder, an excellent cafe where one can purchase sandwiches and home-made cakes at very reasonable prices. If the weather is suitable there is a tea-garden where one may sit out. It is a pleasure to come to Chesters and visitors will go away eminently satisfied with their visit.

# CHAPTER 5

## Chesters to Housesteads and Once Brewed

After leaving Chesters there is a steady climb to the little hamlet of Walwick, where, before the use of modern metalling, the foundations of the Wall often used to be seen in the road surface. As we breast the hill and enter the Northumberland National Park there is a fine view ahead to the west. The ground drops steeply and far in the distance the road can be seen climbing up to Limestone Corner on the skyline. Most impressive of all, there is an excellent stretch of Wall and Ditch running through the common on our right, beside Black Carts Farm.

There are two stretches of Wall here, divided by the road to Simonburn, and this is an area that should be investigated carefully. After inspecting the stretch of Wall containing Turret 29a which lies east of the farm road, one should walk the western section up to the trig point at Limestone Corner. The Wall is well preserved here, rising eight courses high in some places and the Ditch is also particularly fine. On the other side of the Military Road the Vallum is also very well defined as it runs through the wood. The half mile walk takes you through pleasant open countryside with extensive views to the north. As one approaches Limestone Corner the Wall peters out but the gorse-covered Ditch continues to be well defined.

Limestone Corner marks the most northerly point of the Wall. From its wind-blown summit the view to the north over the valley of the North Tyne is magnificent, with Chipchase Castle standing out clearly on its north bank and the Cheviot Hills behind. The rock here is very hard quartz dolerite and the rocks excavated by the Roman engineers lie on the banks of the Ditch. One huge block is still lying in the Ditch and was never removed. Several holes have been cut in its upper surface for the insertion of wedges but the decision must then have been taken to leave it where it was. After rejoining the road by a stile one should pass through a gate on the other side of the road to inspect the Vallum. It is significant that, although the

The Wall and Ditch at Black Carts.

Ditch was left unfinished, the Vallum is everywhere fully dug despite the hardness of the rock. This shows that for the Vallum the ditch was the essential feature, whereas for the Wall it was an extra protection.

From the summit of Limestone Corner the ground drops westwards towards the grassy platform of the fort of Carrawburgh and far in the distance one may see the high crags of the Whin Sill. The Ditch is very prominent here on the right of the road. This is also one of the best places in which to view the Vallum which is outstandingly good as it runs through the fields on the left. The mounds on either side of it may clearly be seen.

The fort at Carrawburgh, whose ancient name was Brocolitia, was comparatively small, occupying about 3½ acres, and was built for an infantry unit of 500 men. It lay across the path of the Vallum, which was filled in to make way for it, and it must have been added comparatively late to the Wall system. Little excavation has been carried out and, although it is possible to distinguish its walls and three of the gateways, the whole fort area is covered in grass. It is fenced off and may be entered by a stile from the roadside car park.

The rock still in position in the Ditch at Limestone Corner.

The fort was brought by John Clayton of Chesters and is still in private hands. While I was making some notes on my last visit a lady came up to me who turned out to be the present owner of the site. She said that the fort would not be excavated in her lifetime, because she wanted to leave something for another generation to discover. She was opposed to a long distance footpath along Hadrian's Wall because she thought there would be a problem of litter and the maintenance of stiles; and she wondered who would compensate the landowners for any damage caused. She brought home to me the need for a responsible attitude if there is to be increased public access to privately owned stretches of Wall country.

The area surrounding the fort was covered by an extensive civilian settlement which is largely unexplored but includes the temple of Mithras discovered in 1949. Mithras was an eastern sun-god, whose cult, that of Good triumphing over Evil, spread rapidly in the Roman world through contacts with the Persian Empire. It was popular in the Roman army and among merchants. Not much is known about the beliefs of his worshippers or of their ritual, although it is thought that animal sacrifice and human initiation by ordeal were included. Of three known Mithraic temples on Hadrian's Wall, this is the only one which is visible. In order to reach the Mithraeum one should go to the gate at the south-east corner of the fort and follow the path round to the temple which lies on lower ground west of the fort. There is an English Heritage notice describing the site with a reconstruction drawing showing what it may have been like. One may compare this drawing with the reconstruction of this temple in the Museum of Antiquities in Newcastle.

The Mithraeum is a long, narrow, stone building, with three altars in the sanctuary at the northern end, one of which has holes pierced through it to enable Mithras' sun-ray crown to be lit up. I well remember my first visit to the site on a cold and dark November afternoon, accompanied by an eccentric sixth form student who lit match after match in an effort to create the desired effect. Inside the entrance there was a small lobby separated from the main body of the temple by a wooden screen. Beyond this there was a central narrow nave, on either side of which lay earthen benches for worshippers. Statues of Mithras' two attendants, Cautes and Cautopates stood on either

The temple of Mithras at Carrawburgh.

side of the nave. The statues, altars and wooden posts now on the site are casts of finds made during excavations in 1949. The originals are in the Museum of Antiquities at Newcastle. The survival of so much of the internal timber was due to the waterlogged conditions of the site.

From the Mithraeum one should pass through a gateway and head north alongside the western rampart of the fort to view a small fenced area on the other side of the field wall. This is the famous Coventina's Well, excavated by John Clayton in 1876. Inside the well he found 13,487 Roman coins and numerous votive offerings which had been thrown there to bring good luck from Coventina, a local water goddess. Most of the finds are now on display in the Chesters Museum, but sadly the well is left in a neglected and overgrown state.

From Carrawburgh the Military Road runs straight for virtually three miles until at last it turns south-west while the Wall with its accompanying Vallum and Ditch goes straight on. This is the point where the road built by General Wade deviates from the Wall, which now runs along the crest of the Whin Sill crags. This is the moment one has been waiting for since leaving Wallsend. It is the start of about 15 miles of rugged country where the Wall survives for much of its length. Motorists should abandon their cars at this point and take to the open country if they wish to appreciate fully the fine remains which are to be seen. The fort of Housesteads lies 2½ miles further west but there is much to see in between which can only be viewed on foot. Unfortunately there is nowhere to park a car here and this section is best seen on a circular walk from Housesteads.

One leaves the road by a little gate beside a footpath sign to Sewingshields. The path follows the line of the Wall and heads for the crest of the ridge. Throughout this section the Vallum is very prominent, and the Ditch survives in a fine condition as far as the start of the crags. Almost immediately on the right lie the remains of Turret 33b (Coesike) which is in a fine state of preservation with its walls standing several courses high. This turret was originally built with short wing walls of Broad gauge but the Wall which eventually joined it was of the Narrow gauge. Like many turrets in this section it only had a short life and by the end of the second century had fallen into disuse and Hadrian's Wall was rebuilt over its ruins. On the north side of the Wall there is a centurial inscription recording work done by the century of Granianus. This is an interesting inscription that may be found by examining the plan which is displayed on the site. The Wall is visible here as a grass-covered mound and the Ditch is in excellent condition.

Continue along the line of the Wall aiming for a clump of trees surrounded by a stone wall. This is the site of Milecastle 34 (Grindon). Just to the west of the milecastle the ground drops steeply away and the Ditch comes to an abrupt end. The countryside was here thought to be so rugged that it was unnecessary to have the Ditch to protect the Wall. Walking through this open windswept country is a delight and this is certainly the best way to approach Housesteads. The ground is rising all the time on the climb towards Sewingshields Crags. Immediately after a stile over a cross wall one comes upon Turret 34a (Grindon). Like other turrets in this section this was thought to have been built by the Twentieth Legion. It too had fallen into disuse by the middle of the second century when the line of the Wall was built over it. From here one passes behind a cottage and across the farm road to a stile giving access to the copse behind Sewingshields Farm.

Shortly after leaving the wood one passes another stretch of wall, consisting mainly of foundations and rubble core. Just short of the crest of the hill there are the well preserved remains of Milecastle 35. Near the trig point on Sewingshields Crags one comes across the remains of Turret 35a. This too was dismantled in the early third century when the Wall was rebuilt over it. This summit of Sewingshields Crags is an outstanding viewpoint with fine views of the crags to the west and of Broomlee and Greenlee Loughs, impressive in their lonely stillness. The path now begins to descend, following the field wall, which was itself built of Wall stones. After passing over a stile one enters a copse and through the trees one may catch a first glimpse of the fort at Housesteads. From the end of the wood a fine section of Wall leads to the north-east corner of the fort.

Before entering Housesteads one should note the Knag Burn gateway, which was inserted in the Wall in the fourth century to allow easier access to the north for the inhabitants of the civil settlement round the fort. Gates were placed at both ends of the passageway, enabling traffic to be stopped and examined before being allowed to pass through. The only traffic I saw on my last visit was a water rat passing through the culvert! The Knag Burn still flows under the Wall in the original Roman culvert just to the left of the gateway.

This route from the east is undoubtedly the finest approach to Housesteads. From this angle one has a clear view of the fort and can appreciate the impressive height to which its walls survive. I came this way late one summer's evening. It was just at dusk and I was the only one on the site. I had the feeling I was trespassing on Roman military premises and felt rather guilty creeping through the west gate without asking for permission. I rapidly made my way to the south gate and hurried through the vicus and down the hill to the car-park, leaving the fort and its environs to the sheep who are now its only inhabitants.

Housesteads is the best preserved fort on the Wall and probably the most popular. Beside the Military Road the National Trust have provided a large car-park and shop, from which one climbs to the fort by a path through the fields. The fort itself is in the care of English Heritage. Alongside the site there is a small museum which contains a model of the fort and the civil settlement as it may have looked in the third century. There is a life-size model of a second century auxiliary soldier and several finds from the site are also displayed. Panels round the walls provide valuable information about Roman Britain, the building of Hadrian's Wall, the history of the fort and civil settlement, and details of the Roman Army. There is also a collection of drawings by the artist Ronald Embleton that depict various scenes from Roman life. School parties may use an education room in one of the farm buildings.

The fort at Housesteads was added to the Wall within a few years of its construction in AD 122. It was not possible for the fort to lie across the Wall, which here runs along the edge of the crags, and so it was sited with its main entrance facing east and with one of its long sides parallel to the line of the Wall. The fort is laid out according to the normal design. In the centre lay the headquarters building (principia), the granaries, and the commanding officer's house (praetorium). Behind the principia was a courtyard building normally identified as a hospital and at each end of the fort lay barracks, stables and workshops.

The name of the fort in Roman times is not exactly clear but seems to have been either Vercovicium or Borcovicium. The garrison for much of the fort's life was the First Cohort of Tungrians, a 1000 strong regiment originally recruited from the area around what is now Tongeren in eastern Belgium. Later units based here included Frisian cavalry (from Holland), and a unit of irregular German troops.

Before entering the fort it is a good idea to walk a little way round the outside in order to appreciate the massive walls that still stand to a considerable height. One should then enter by the south gate and make one's way uphill to the north gate on the crest of the ridge so as to view the whole site from above. English Heritage have placed excellent notices, often accompanied by reconstruction drawings, at all the major features.

The north gate was originally planned with a double entrance and its western gateway showed considerable signs of wear, indicating that wagons had used it for a long period of time. There was an external stone ramp allowing it to be used despite

The north granary at Housesteads.

the steep slope, but this was removed by the excavators in 1853. 30 yards to the west of the gate lie the exposed foundations of Turret 36b. This was built before the decision was taken to place forts on the line of the Wall and had to be demolished to make way for the construction of the fort.

A little to the south lie the remains of two very fine granaries. They were buttressed in order to bear the great weight of the stored corn and to support the heavy roof. The rows of piers which are visible carried the joists of a wooden floor which covered a ventilated basement. This was to ensure good ventilation for the stored food and to deter vermin. There were probably loading platforms at the western end, to which carts could be brought for unloading grain. At some time in the 17th century a large malt-kiln was inserted into the central portion of the south granary.

Further to the east lie the remains of two large barrack blocks which have been excavated comparatively recently. When first built these followed the normal pattern of a long building divided into 10 rooms for the soldiers of a century (80 men), with larger quarters for the centurion at the eastern end. The

71

remains visible today date mainly from the fourth century when the barrack rooms were replaced by six individual houses, a workshop and the centurion's suite. These houses may have been married quarters for individual soldiers and their families. The east gate was the main entrance to the fort and from it a street led directly to the headquarters building. The gateway was originally planned, like all the others, with two passages, but at a later date the south passage was walled up and the space used as an extra guard room. The former guard room was converted into a coal store and in 1833 nearly a cart load of coal was found in this area. Wheel ruts eight inches deep, which are cut in the threshold of the north passage, show that there was much traffic through this gate. These ruts, like those at Pompeii, are very close to the British railway gauge and local legend has it that George Stephenson took his gauge from this gateway. But it seems that some years before these gates were uncovered Stephenson decided on his gauge by averaging the wheel gauge of 100 carts. The Military Way, the road which connected the forts on the Wall, ran straight up to this gateway, and left the fort by the west gate.

In the angle tower at the south-east and lowest corner of the fort lie what are probably the most famous remains at Housesteads, the latrines. The entrance to these was from the west, and there was a central platform with wooden seats set over deep channels along the sides of the building. The stone channel in front of the seats carried water for washing sponges, which were the Roman equivalent of toilet paper, and there is a stone basin at one end for washing hands. Running water flushed the channels and flowed through a sewer under the fort rampart to discharge further down the hillside. Much of this water will have been provided by the rainwater which was stored in tanks like that seen beside the angle tower nearby. It is not clear what alternative water supply was available. Some forts on the Wall had elaborate aqueducts bringing fresh spring water to them but there are no traces of these at Housesteads. These latrines are well preserved and considered one of the finest military examples north of the Alps. They illustrate the importance attached by the Roman army to the hygiene of its soldiers. One should view Ronald Emberton's

The latrines at Housesteads.

excellent reconstruction to get a vivid view of how these toilets were used. It is clear that they had something of the communal atmosphere of the bathhouse, strange though this may seem to modern sensitivities!

Although the south gate is the one most used today, it was not the main entrance to the fort in Roman days. Like the other gates it was planned to be a double gateway, flanked by twin guardchambers, but later the eastern entrance was walled up. The pivot-holes for the doors can be clearly seen. The building which lies against the south face of the gateway is a 16th century fortified farmhouse. It had a vaulted basement below and the upper living quarters were approached by an external stair on the east side. At a later date the east guard chamber of the gateway itself was converted into a kiln to dry corn.

The west gate is the finest of Housesteads gateways and survives up to the base of the archway. The holes for the bar which was slotted into place after the gates were closed are clearly visible. The gateway originally had two entrances with guardchambers on either side. Both gateways were later

The west gate at Housesteads.

blocked and the whole gate was then filled with a solid mass of rubble so that the fort rampart ran continuously through. This filling was removed at the time of excavation. The western rampart on either side of the west gate is excellently preserved and still stands 11 courses high.

One should now approach the central buildings of the fort, starting with the headquarters building (principia) which was approached from the eastern end. This was the very heart of the fort and its appearance was suitably impressive. Its main entrance was originally a monumental doorway adorned with a statue of Mars, the Roman god of war. This led to an open courtyard flanked by a colonnade. Directly ahead was a further doorway into a large hall set across the whole width of the building. In the hall was a platform (tribunal) on which the commanding officer stood to dispense military justice and to preside over parades. On the far side of the hall there is a series of five rooms. The central one was the chapel where the garrison's standards and the image of the reigning emperor were kept. Other rooms were used as regimental offices.

The stone buildings that are visible today date from the third century. Beneath these buildings lie the remains of the original headquarters building, which was constructed when the fort was first built in about AD 125. Later in the fort's history, the headquarters building underwent various changes which closed in the open colonnade and converted parts of the office space into domestic quarters.

The building immediately to the west of the principia is thought to be a hospital (valetudinarium). Courtyard buildings of this type in Roman forts are usually identified as hospitals and the probability of this being correct at Housesteads is supported by the discovery here of the tombstone of a soldier called Anicius Ingenuus of the 1st Cohort of Tungrians who is described as a doctor (medicus). He died at the age of 25. The building consists of small rooms each with a narrow passageway set round a central courtyard, which originally contained a verandah. These small rooms may have been wards. Drainage channels are visible and there is a latrine in the south wing. After the removal of the verandah, the central courtyard was extended and re-surfaced with flagstones.

To the south of the headquarters building lies the commanding officer's house (praetorium). This was a large courtyard house similar to Roman town houses found in Pompeii and elsewhere. The main residential quarters consisted of a kitchen with a large oven, a dining area, and a suite of domestic rooms. The stone pillars which supported the floor allowed heated air to pass under the paved floor and up through channels in the walls. A solid gold signet ring was found in the latrine in the western range. In the southern part of the house on the lower side of the hill were servants' quarters and a stable with a paved floor. The building has gone through several modifications during its occupation.

Outside the fort, to the south and east, lay the remains of a considerable civil settlement (vicus). Troops with regular incomes and money to spare provided a ready market and such settlements of traders grew up outside most Roman forts. The extensive remains of a temple to Mithras are now displayed in the Museum of Antiquities at Newcastle, and it is known that there was also a temple to Mars Thincsus. Earthworks, cultivation terraces, and house platforms cover a wide area

The north gate of Milecastle 37 (Housesteads).

around the fort. A few of these buildings are visible today just outside the south gate. Two of them have produced dramatic finds. One yielded evidence that coins had been counterfeited there and was evidently a coiners' den. Below the floor of another building two skeletons were found buried in the rear room. One was probably a woman and the other was a middle-aged man with the point of a sword still lodged between his ribs. This is clearly the scene of a murder, for burials were not permitted within a Roman settlement.

Housesteads is an outstanding example of a Roman fort and its remains evoke a clear picture of the past. Set in a glorious hillside setting there is much for the visitor to see and the site is well maintained by English Heritage. The fort lies at the eastern end of the best preserved section of the Wall and from it there are fine walks to view the various features of the Wall system.

One should leave the fort by its north-west corner and walk on the top of the Wall through Housesteads Wood, a pleasant copse of sycamore, ash and Scots pine. In early summer there is a profusion of wild flowers: buttercups, clover, harebells, and foxgloves towering over beds of fern. To the north there is an extensive view over bare pastureland to the grim confines of the vast Wark Forest.

On emerging from the wood one immediately comes upon the site of Milecastle 37 (Housesteads). This is one of the best preserved milecastles on the Wall and was excavated by John Clayton in 1852, with further work being carried out in 1907 and 1933. Part of an inscription found here shows that it was built by the Second Legion. The large stones out of which its gates were built are typical of the work of that legion. The north gate is particularly well preserved with three stones of the arch in position on either side. The north wall of the milecastle is at least 15 courses high in the north-west corner, making it the highest standing piece of original masonry on the Wall. The foundations of the north gate were built to Broad gauge but the curtain walls which joined it were of Narrow gauge and they taper on either side of the gate, a feature unique to this milecastle. The remains of a stone-built barrack block, large enough to have housed eight men are located in the eastern half. 50 yards to the west of the milecastle one may clearly identify a joining of two different thicknesses of the Wall where the work of two legionary working parties met.

From the milecastle a path runs beside the Wall, which here is uniformly seven courses high; it dips into a hollow and climbs the hillside, which is known as Cuddy's Crags. Cuddy is a local name for St Cuthbert, who was closely associated with the north. On reaching the top of the hill one should turn back and look eastwards for what is probably the most famous of all views of the Wall, as it climbs the slope and enters Housesteads Wood.

The path continues westwards beside the Wall which here is in fine condition and rises about six courses high. 50 yards or so to the south, the Military Way can easily be picked out as it runs through a succession of field gates. The ground drops sharply to Rapishaw Gap which is reached by a steep but satisfying climb down rocks, which may be bypassed on the south by those who prefer a gentler descent. From the gap a footpath sign indicates where the Pennine Way (which has been following the line of the Wall for several miles from the west) heads northwards over the fields to enter the eastern end of Wark Forest.

The Wall at Cuddy's Crags.

The restored lime kiln south of Rapishaw Gap.

Those who have surplus energy and an interest in lime kilns may here wish to detour from the line of the Wall. 500 yards due south from Rapishaw Gap is a kiln which has been well preserved by the National Trust. There is another kiln, also in fine condition, 600 yards north of the Wall. Those who make the digression north will get a clear impression of the crags on which the Wall lies and will gain a better understanding of the rugged nature of the country.

There is a stiff climb from Rapishaw Gap up to Hotbank Crags, with steps assisting one's progress in the steepest section. After a short absence the Wall reappears at the top of the crags and is uniformly six courses high. From the summit of Hotbank Crags there are fine views in every direction. A copse north of the Wall on the edge of the crags provides shelter for Hotbank Farm which nestles in the hollow below. As the ridge descends to Milking Gap there are increasingly fine views of the lovely Crag Lough which lies ahead beneath the sheer cliffs of Highshield Crags. Just below Hotbank Farm the grassy outlines of Milecastle 38 (Hotbank) may be seen. Inscriptions

The Wall on Hotbank Crags with Crag Lough in the background.

recording that it was built by men of the Second Legion were originally set up over both the north and south gates. One of these inscriptions may be seen in the Museum of Antiquities at Newcastle.

From Milking Gap one may follow the farm road left to join the Military Road. If one is returning to Housesteads the best and most varied route would be to follow the Military Way which runs parallel to the Wall and south of it, passing through a series of field gates until it reaches the west gate of Housesteads fort. For those wishing to visit Vindolanda (the famous fort on the Stanegate which lies just over a mile south of the Wall) there is an excellent route over the fields from Hotbank Farm. A footpath sign indicates the path which runs diagonally south-west to cross the Military Road and pass to the left of High Shield Farm. After crossing a wall by a stile continue downhill to Vindolanda which can be seen below. The path emerges by the Roman milestone on the Stanegate just beside the entrance to the Vindolanda Museum.

From Hotbank Farm the line of the Wall resumes its westward course, climbing through a wood and on to the summit of

Crag Lough with Hotbank Crags on the skyline.

Highshield Crags, where the Wall may be seen south of the path in an unconserved state covered with grass. This is a delightful spot. In early summer celandines, violets and wood-sorrel grow in profusion and jackdaws fly incessantly from their nests at the top of the crags. The graceful presence of a pair of swans adds to the wild beauty of the lough and a fisherman's boat is sometimes to be seen drifting slowly across its lonely waters. Notices here warn of the presence of toxic algae in Crag Lough, a sad reminder of the ever-present natural dangers to our environment. Ahead the view is dominated by Winshields Crags, the highest point on the Wall, and below, in a little cluster of trees, lies the Steel Rigg car-park. This is majestically wild and lonely country matched in its magnificence only by the uncompromising grandeur of the Wall itself.

The Wall survives in excellent condition, rising to seven courses high in places, as the path drops into the aptly named Sycamore Gap, dominated by a magnificent sycamore tree. It is pleasing to note that a tiny replacement sycamore sapling is making good progress within a small walled enclosure. This spot will be familiar to many as the opening scene in the highly

Milecastle 39 (Castle Nick).

successful 1991 film *Robin Hood, Prince of Thieves*. There is a fine
stepped section of Wall as it climbs the hill out of the gap. On
this hillside there are stone remains of two shielings, shelters
for shepherds tending their sheep on summer pastures. It is
from the word shieling that the numerous names ending in
Shield in this area are derived. In the next gap lies the
finely preserved Milecastle 39 (Castle Nick). Its walls stand
four or five courses high and there are traces of barrack
blocks.

On the top of Peel Crags there is an excellent section of
Wall, much of it six courses high. This is possibly the finest
continuous stretch on the line of the Wall. This section was
excavated and restored by F. G. Simpson in 1909–11, and in
the course of this work Turret 39a was discovered, the only
known example of a Narrow gauge turret. It was constructed
in the first phase of Wall building and it fell into disuse later
in the second century.

The Wall comes to an abrupt end at the western end of Peel
Crags and care is needed as one follows the steep path down

the cliffs, although this section of the route has recently been made safer for pedestrians. The Wall resumes again at the foot of the crags at Peel Gap and there is a good stretch that has been recently excavated; the remains of what seems to have been an extra tower have been discovered. The path crosses a boggy section by a planked way and climbs a grassy slope to rejoin the Wall. On my last visit National Trust workmen were repairing a section of the Wall which had collapsed during the winter because of frost damage. This was in a stretch which had been inadequately conserved in the last century.

If returning to Housesteads from Peel Gap there is no need to retrace one's steps along the Wall. There is a very fine walk which takes one north of the Wall and rejoins the ridge east of Housesteads, a distance of about $3\frac{1}{2}$ miles. From the Steel Rigg car-park go 200 yards north-west along the road before picking up a footpath running eastwards which is signposted to Hotbank. This route provides a fine view of the crags over which the Wall runs. One can see that they really are precipitous rock cliffs and appreciate the significance of the gaps that sheer through them at Castle Nick and Sycamore Gap. This is indeed a native's view of the Wall and with a little imagination the figures of walkers on the Wall against the skyline may easily be taken for Roman soldiers. Voices come clearly over the air as must those of the Romans before them. The wide expanse of open country north of the Wall gives one the strange feeling of being beyond known territory, of being in some strange way deprived of the familiar protection provided by the Wall.

The path runs north of Hotbank Farm and, after passing the lime kiln north of Rapishaw Gap and crossing the Pennine Way, it follows the line of crags eastwards. There are fine views of Cuddy's and Housesteads Crags and one also gets an unusual view of the fort wall and north gate of Housesteads. After passing through a small plantation the path climbs up to join the ridge at King's Wicket. From here one heads westwards over King's Hill, Clew Hill and Kennel Crags to pass through the wood to Housesteads fort.

An interesting alternative is to return to Housesteads by the Military Way. It is an excellent route to follow for, by the nature of its purpose, it seeks out the easiest gradient, avoiding many of the ups and downs of the Wall without actually deviating very far from its line. It is also very easy to follow since small field gates usually accompanied by a stile, take it through all the cross walls.

The Military Way appears as a broad grassy swathe covering a paved stony surface as it sweeps round the southern end of Peel Crags. Below Highshield Crags and in the stretch from Sycamore Gap to Milking Gap it is in a particularly fine condition and over 15 feet wide in several places. For most of its route it runs about 100 yards south of the Wall and provides most pleasant walking. It passes to the south of Milecastle 37 (Housesteads) and leads to the west gate of Housesteads fort.

If you wish to avoid the crowds thronging the Wall, the Military Way often provides a quiet alternative which is equally evocative. It was raining on the last occasion I walked this stretch. I only had the sheep for company but I felt that I was also accompanied by the ghosts of generations of Roman soldiers who must often have tramped this way.

# CHAPTER 6

## *Once Brewed to Vindolanda and Carvoran*

The National Park Information Centre at Once Brewed is a pleasant modern building on the south side of the Military Road opposite the approach to Peel Gap. It lies in a cluster of buildings servicing the needs of Wall visitors, including the Twice Brewed Inn, the Once Brewed Youth Hostel and the Vallum Lodge Hotel. The Centre is a busy place and on a recent Spring Bank Holiday Monday had over 1000 visitors. The Northumberland National Park covers 398 square miles of mainly hill country and includes many acres of remote, thinly-populated moorland and also large areas of forest. The Centre provides valuable facilities for visitors. Books and maps may be purchased and light refreshments are available. A warden is on hand to give advice and one may watch a range of videos dealing with the historical and topographical interest of the area. Leaflets are also available describing some of the suggested walking routes. There is a car-park and a picnic area.

The fort of Vindolanda lies on the Stanegate, the Roman road linking the forts of the pre-Hadrianic frontier, and is just over a mile south of the Wall. The walker on the Wall may approach the site by a footpath which runs south from Milking Gap. The motorist has the choice of two routes. The best approach to appreciate the strategic situation of Vindolanda is to turn south off the Military Road one mile west of Housesteads, on the road to Bardon Mill. After passing the remains of a very well-preserved lime kiln, one turns right at a T junction to pass under the hill of Barcombe. Take the first turning right (banned to coaches) which leads to Vindolanda's eastern car-park. As you approach the car-park you have a fine view of the fort and civil settlement on the slope facing you and are able to gain a good idea of the strategic nature of the site, with the fort occupying a grassy plateau overlooking the Chineley Burn. This was once the main approach to Vindolanda, but hardly anyone seems to use it nowadays.

The normal approach, and the only one permitted for coaches, is to turn south beside the Once Brewed Information Centre and to take the first road to the left. This brings one straight to the western car-park of the fort. This route has the advantage of taking you down the line of the Stanegate, but it conveys little idea of the strategic position of the fort. Entering from the west, however, enables you to view the site in a logical sequence, passing through the civil settlement first, before examining the fort and completing one's visit at the museum and coffee shop.

Vindolanda is a unique site for several reasons. Although the actual fort is in the care of English Heritage, the site as a whole is owned and administered by the Vindolanda Trust, an independent charitable Trust founded in 1970 for the excavation and preservation of this important site. Unlike most forts on the Wall interest centres mainly on the civil settlement rather than on the fort, and this is where excavations are currently being carried out. Some of the most outstanding finds in Roman Britain have been made here, including the famous wooden writing tablets. Replicas of some of the main features of the Wall system have been erected here and the site also has a superb museum set in charming gardens. This is by far the best museum on the Wall and one is not surprised to learn that in 1990 the magazine *Holiday Which* voted it 'Best Site Museum in Britain'.

On leaving the western car-park one immediately enters the civilian settlement. A useful feature is provided by the two listening posts, where by pressing a button one is given a commentary first on the civil settlement and then on the fort, and reference is made to some of the outstanding finds now on display in the museum. A prominent building with a rounded apse on the left of the path is a military bath house. These were normally built outside the fort walls in order to save space and to prevent a risk of fire. They were also available for use by civilians, and in the drains of this bath house hairpins, combs, beads and the remains of a small sandal have been found. One should note the hypocaust pillars on which the floors were raised to enable hot air from the stoke holes to circulate. There is a small latrine in the north-east corner.

The Military bath house at Vindolanda.

In front of the military bath house lie the remains of several civilian houses. The first of these is known as a corridor house. This was a large building with rooms opening off a central corridor. At some stage its front room seems to have been converted into a butcher's shop. The stone base of the serving counter can be seen and the floor of the shop has a triple drain system to carry away animal blood into the main town drain which runs in front of the building. When the house was excavated large quantities of pale green window-glass were discovered. The house next door is a long rectangular house known as a strip house. An owner was taxed according to the amount of street frontage his house occupied, and so only the narrow part of a strip house faced on to the street.

On the right of the path is a large building which was an inn for travellers (mansio). It is built around a large open courtyard, on each side of which are three bedrooms. A gutter runs round the courtyard to catch rainwater from the roof. There was a small heated dining room with a kitchen next door. The inn also had a small bath suite equipped with a latrine which had eight wooden seats round the sides of the room. There would have been buckets

The replicas at Vindolanda. On the right is a turret and on the left a milecastle gateway in the Turf Wall.

under the seats which required emptying daily.

Other buildings in the settlement include soldiers' married quarters and metal workshops. Alongside the replica buildings there are some remains of a cemetery. This must have been outside the limits of the settlement because in Roman times it was forbidden to bury people inside a town.

The replicas dominate the site from all angles. They were constructed in 1973–74 by senior pupils from Heathfield High School, Gateshead, assisted by the staff of Vindolanda. The aim was to demonstrate the size of the Wall and to discover the problems of its construction. It is interesting to note that their most difficult task was digging the Ditch. The most imposing structure is the reconstruction of a section of the stone wall together with a turret. In a corner of the turret, wooden stairs resting on a stone platform give access to the first storey and the Wall walkway. Scholars still argue over the final dimensions of the Wall and whether there was a crenellated parapet. These reconstructions were based on the best evidence available and certainly convey a clear impression of the massive structure of the Wall system.

Excavations in progress during 1991 under the direction of Robin Birley.

The western sector of the Wall was originally built in turf and a section of the Turf Wall, together with the timber gateway of a milecastle, has been built adjoining the stone Wall. You may climb by interior stairs up to the top storey to gain a fine breezy view over the whole site. Since its construction the Turf Wall has settled considerably and lost over three feet of its height. In the centre of the replica buildings is a reconstruction of a Roman ballista. This was a weapon capable of throwing large stones, metal bolts and arrows over a considerable distance. There are examples of ballista bolts in the museum.

The current excavation area lies just south of the fort's east gate. There is a programme of excavations each year and since 1973 many fascinating discoveries have been made, chief among them the remarkable Vindolanda writing tablets. It is now known that there were at least five timber forts on the site before the first stone fort was built in AD 140. Because the Romans sealed the remains of disused buildings with a layer of turf before rebuilding on the site, the remains of wooden posts and other debris from the earlier forts have been protected from oxygen and kept at an even temperature. This has enabled the preservation of leather, wooden and metal objects, and even of textiles, in excellent condition. The remarkable finds made here are now displayed in the museum. '

Vindolanda started life as a timber fort in about AD 80, as one of a series of forts along the line of the Stanegate. It seems to have been temporarily abandoned at the time when Hadrian's Wall was being built and then to have been rebuilt in stone about AD 163 as part of the Wall frontier system. Its garrison at one time was the Fourth Cohort of Gauls, a part-mounted regiment of 500 men. The fort occupies a prominent raised platform dominating the Chineley Burn and covers 3.5 acres.

The headquarters building is a particularly fine example. It was entered from the north and the rooms on either side of the entrance were storerooms. There is a well over 20 feet deep in the open courtyard in which the excavators found the skulls of ten oxen. The cross-hall was a large area in which the whole regiment could assemble, at the western end of which is the raised platform (tribunal) used by the commanding officer. Along the back of the cross-hall lies a suite of five rooms, the central one of which was the chapel of the standards, where the regimental standards and a statue of the emperor would have been kept. Behind this room there is a sunken strong-room where the pay and savings and all the other valuables of the regiment would have been deposited. The rooms on either side were offices where military clerks dealt with the administration of the regiment.

The fort walls survive in very good condition and are several feet high in places. The north and west gates are well preserved. Both had single passageways with guard rooms on either side. In the north-east corner of the fort a small latrine block has been excavated. This had timber seating and could probably have accommodated six persons at a time.

From the fort one should follow the path eastwards over the fast-flowing Chineley Burn and through the beautiful gardens to the museum. On the terrace outside the museum there is a memorial to all the regiments who are known to have served at Vindolanda in the period AD 85–400.

Before entering the museum you should walk on to the Stanegate (the farm road behind the museum building) to view

The Roman milestone on the Stanegate at Vindolanda.

the Roman milestone opposite Codley Gate Farm. It stands over five feet high and has found its way into the *Guinness Book of Records* as the only Roman milestone in Britain still standing to its full height in its original position. On your return to the museum do not fail to greet one of the many cats you will see basking in the sunshine. Last time I was there I saw five of them. These cats lead a semi-wild existence surviving on sandwiches and titbits from visitors, but they look sleek and comfortable and are very friendly.

The museum at Vindolanda is most impressive. It lies in a lovely setting and it houses a composite collection from both the fort and the civil settlement, including some of the most remarkable finds ever discovered in Roman Britain. There is an attractive coffee shop and a book shop offering a wide range of books, pamphlets and souvenirs for sale. A fully comprehensive pack for teachers is also available.

There are eight display rooms and also a small film theatre where one may view the film *Vindolanda's Wooden Underworld*, which tells the story of the remarkable discovery of the writing

The reconstructed Roman kitchen at Vindolanda.

tablets. In one room there is an excellent audio-visual display of a Roman kitchen. Materna, whose husband Marcus is serving with the army in the fort, gives a woman's view of life in a typical family in the civil settlement. She is 26 and has had six children of whom four survive. Included in the display is her young son Victor, her baby daughter Ursa and the pet dog Lupulus (Little Wolf), formerly a hunting dog. She describes her daily life in the settlement and how her family help her. This is an excellent display which manages to avoid artificiality and hits just the right note of realism. There is even a hint of pathos when she talks of her hopes for her children.

There is a very fine display of finds from the early wooden forts on the site. This includes many wooden objects, pegs, boxes, a gate, parts of wagon wheels, and even a trestle table-top. One cabinet displays a variety of Roman tools including a selection of keys and locks, knives, shoe studs, a branding iron, tongs, lead weights, an entrenching tool, a bucket handle and a chisel. It is also interesting to see wooden tent pegs of a type in regular use until comparatively recent times. There is also a fine collection of Pre–Hadrianic iron fitments including weapon heads, a sword blade, a dagger, stone shot and lead sling bullets.

Remains of a wide variety of Roman animals have been found showing that Roman soldiers were not vegetarians as was once thought. Traces of goat, horse, boar, deer, oxen and dog have been found on the site, and there is an interesting comparison of ancient and modern chicken bones.

In addition to an extensive collection of Roman pottery, there is a fascinating display of textiles, showing the results of experiments in the use of Roman dyes and traditional weaving methods. There is also a cabinet devoted to the cosmetics and hair fashions of Roman women, showing wooden combs, rings, brooches, hairpins, tweezers to pluck eyebrows, a silver dress fastener and even a woman's hair piece.

Several thousand pieces of leather have been excavated from Vindolanda's pre-Hadrianic levels during the last few years and one cabinet has an amazing display of leatherwork, showing numerous sandals, shoes and slippers, including one with the owner's name stamped on it. There are even pieces of a leather tent with edging strips, patches, thongs and fastenings all clearly visible.

But the most fascinating collection of all is that of the Vindolanda writing tablets. When the Romans covered the remains of earlier buildings with turf they created the damp, oxygen-free environment which was essential for the preservation of timber, leather, textiles and writing tablets. These tablets are thin wafers of wood, no more than 1 millimetre thick, which, when photographed by infra-red film, reveal traces of Roman writing. These tablets date from the period AD 80–125. They are written in cursive script, a forerunner of modern handwriting. There is no punctuation and they are not easy to read. Over 1000 writing tablets have been found since 1972. They include private correspondence, official reports and lists of stores.

One document, discovered in May 1988, was the annual report to the governor giving details of the strength of the First Cohort of Tungrians, the first garrison at Vindolanda in about AD 90. Its commander was the prefect Julius Verecundius and, out of its 750 men and six centuries, some 450 men and five centurions were absent. It lists the reasons for their absence. Some were serving in the body guard of the governor of the province or on the staff of the procurator (the financial officer). Others were on duty at a fort named as Coria, which is probably Corbridge. Only 270 men and one centurion remained at Vindolanda and of these more than 10 per cent were unfit for duty. Some were listed as wounded, while others were suffering from conjunctivitis (pink-eye).

Another document consists of an invitation to Sulpicia Lepedina, the wife of Flavius Cerialis, prefect of the Ninth Cohort of Batavians, the garrison at Vindolanda in about AD 100, to attend the birthday party of her friend Claudia Severa. There is also what appears to be part of an intelligence report which describes the poor fighting qualities of the native British and refers to them as Brittunculi, 'the wretched Britons'. Also, written in capital letters on the back of a discarded letter, is line 473 from Book IX of Virgil's Aeneid. This is probably a writing exercise done by one of Cerialis' children, who are referred to elsewhere in the tablets as being at Vindolanda with their mother. There is also part of a letter written to a soldier at Vindolanda which reads: 'I have sent you . . . pairs of socks, two pairs of sandals and two sets of underpants'!

There is a tableau explaining Roman methods of writing and showing a scribe writing on a wooden tablet. He is using thin, flat pieces of wood smoothed to take writing in ink on one or both sides. The pen is a hard reed sharpened at one end, and the ink contained water, lamp black and gum. Several tablets could be joined in a concertina fashion by thongs. An alternative method of writing was by using a metal sharp-pointed stylus pen on recessed pieces of wood coated with wax. Records of these have survived because the pen often penetrated into the wood leaving behind traces of the message long after the wax disappeared.

No trip to Vindolanda is complete without making the ascent of Barcombe, the bracken and heather covered hill which lies to the south-east, and which is notable for the Long Stone prominently visible on its ridge. From the eastern car park walk up to the T junction and turn left. After just over half a mile a stile on the right gives access to a path providing a diagonal and gentle ascent to the ridge. A footpath sign beside

The Long Stone on Barcombe with the fort of Vindolanda and the Chineley Burn below.

the stile indicates Thorngrafton 1 mile. This path is marked on the map and clearly seen on the ground. It gains the summit ridge midway between the trig point and the Long Stone.

The Long Stone commemorates the tragic death of a quarryman in the 18th century. From this vantage point there is a magnificent view in all directions. To the north-west there is a fine aerial view of Vindolanda and the Stanegate running in a straight line beyond it. You can appreciate the strategic position of the fort on a level platform above the Chineley Burn, and the size of the replicas makes one realise how the Wall must have dominated the landscape. The close relationship of the vicus to the fort is also clearly apparent. There is a fine view of Housesteads to the north-east, while eastwards the Stanegate snakes away in the direction of Corbridge.

After visiting the trig point one should cross to the northern spur of the ridge where a circular earthwork with clearly visible grass banks reveals the site of a native pre-Roman hill fort. Just south of this settlement a small hollow circular mound marks

The summit of Winshields Crags 1230 feet. The highest point of the Wall.

the site of a Roman signal station. There are many small quarries on Barcombe and one of them is said still to bear traces of Roman graffiti, although I have been unable to find it. In 1837 a Roman bronze purse with three gold coins and 60 silver coins in it was found in the cleft of an old working face of one of the quarries.

After visiting Vindolanda one should return to the Steel Rigg car-park at Peel Gap and prepare for the ascent of Winshields Crags, whose summit at 1230 feet marks the highest point on the Wall. A signpost directs one westwards to Shield on the Wall and gives a reminder that for the next few miles we are on the Pennine Way. The line of the Wall follows the field wall up the slope, past the grassy mounds of Turret 39b (Steel Rigg), excavated by F. G. Simpson in 1911. Like many of the turrets in the central sector of the Wall it was dismantled at the end of the second century and the Wall was rebuilt across it. The Ditch now reappears and accompanies one for a considerable way up the slope until the crags render it unnecessary.

From the summit of Winshields Crags there are spectacular views of wild and lonely country in all directions. But apart from one or two stretches of rough unconsolidated wall, there are few visible remains. From the trig point a series of short climbs and steep descents brings one to the Caw Gap and the lonely farm of Shield on the Wall. To the north lies the solitary house of Burn Deviot, which used to be a haunt of smugglers and sheepstealers. According to local tradition lights are seen to flicker at night in the house, indicating the presence of the spirits of those murdered there. The Wall begins immediately after leaving the gap and continues without a break in a good state of preservation over Cawfield Crags. After passing the foundations of Turret 41a there is a particularly fine stretch rising to 13 courses in places. This is good walking country. In summer lapwings fly overhead and the plaintive cry of the curlew may frequently be heard.

After crossing the ominously named Bloody Gap one comes across the excellently preserved remains of Milecastle 42 (Cawfields). This was excavated by John Clayton in 1848 and has gates of a pattern which is normally associated with the Second Legion. A fragment of a building inscription of Hadrianic date was discovered and also part of a tombstone of a Pannonian soldier reused as a hearth. The north gate and adjoining portions of the Wall were found to have been built before the rest of the milecastle, showing that the sites of milecastles were measured out at an early stage of the building programme.

It is sad to note that this excellent stretch of Wall comes to an abrupt end at the sheer walls of the Cawfields Quarry which has here destroyed a considerable section. The quarry has now been bought out by the nation but the visitor is left to lament the irreplaceable loss to our national heritage. One should pause here to admire what is probably the best preserved stretch of Vallum over the whole length of the Wall. At Cawfields car-park there are toilets and, during the season, a mobile snack bar specialising in home cooking including excellent fruit cake. There is ample space for parking and also an attractive picnic site.

From Cawfields one crosses the fast-flowing Haltwhistle Burn, where in 1908 excavators found the site of a Roman water-mill. A footpath notice beside a stile indicates the route westwards. The path leads across a field aiming for the highest point of the crag. There has been no trace of the Wall since the quarry,

The Wall on Cawfield Crags.

Milecastle 42 (Cawfields).

but the Ditch now appears on the other side of a field wall. The path continues ahead keeping the field wall on one's right and gradually traces of Wall can be seen in the grassy mound underlying the field wall.

The Ditch continues to be prominent as one approaches the fort of Aesica beside Greatchesters Farm. The fort's grassy platform may easily be picked out but the visible remains are not extensive. The path runs left of the farm and makes for a stile beside the fort's grass-covered eastern rampart. Aesica covers an area of three acres and, like Carrawburgh, lay entirely south of the Wall. It faces east and its prime function was to guard the Caw Gap. In the 18th century its walls were said to stand 12 or 13 feet high, but today only low traces of its west and south walls remain. The west gate is of special interest to archaeologists because it is the only gate on the Wall which still has intact the various blocking walls by which it was reduced first to one gateway and then finally closed altogether.

Limited excavations were conducted in 1894 when a hoard of jewellery was found in the west tower of the south gate.

The Wall and the Vallum at Cawfields. Milecastle 42 may also be seen.

Amongst the items was the famous gilded bronze Aesica Brooch, which has been described as a masterpiece of Celtic art. A replica may be seen in the Museum of Antiquities at Newcastle. A fenced-off area in the centre contains the vaulted arch of the fort's underground strong room, a particularly fine example of this feature. The fort of Aesica lies in a pleasing pastoral setting and its deserted ruins leave one with a vague impression of lonely splendour.

From the fort a series of stiles takes one past the farmhouse of Cockmount Hill and climbs a grassy slope to the highest point of the hill. The Ditch appears intermittently and there are occasional traces of the lowest courses of the Wall. This is pleasant walking over an open grassy common, with the path following the field wall which itself stands on Wall foundations. In this section the crags are broken by the frequent gaps known as the Nine Nicks of Thirlwell. It is interesting to note how the Wall covers each of these gaps by turning sharply south then veering north before resuming its westward course. On Mucklebank Crag, Turret 44b lies in an angle of the Wall, splendidly placed with a steep drop below. Its walls are about seven courses high and, because of its position, both its north and west sides are recessed into the Wall. After crossing the farm road at Walltown Nick we begin the ascent of Walltown Crags.

At first the Wall is seen as a grass-covered mound with the occasional stone protruding, but as the ridge gains height the Wall emerges again and for 150 yards to the quarry edge is four courses high and excellently preserved. But unfortunately this fine stretch has been terminated by the activities of Walltown quarry. The Wall ends abruptly at the eastern edge of the quarry and the path veers left, protected from the sheer drop by a fence. Immediately to the west of the quarry the Wall starts again and its next section is outstandingly good. Turret 45a is well-preserved and is especially interesting because it seems initially to have been a free-standing tower before the Wall was built. The Wall butts to its east and west sides, showing that it is a later construction. It may originally have been a watch tower linking up with the signalling tower at Pike Hill further to the west.

The Wall here is very well preserved and this is probably

The Wall on Walltown Crags.

the finest to be seen anywhere along its line. Not only is it at least nine courses high rising to a height of five feet, but it also is in an excellent state of preservation. It is particularly interesting to see the way in which it ascends and descends the steep inclines, incorporating rocks into its path, sometimes following the slope of the land and in other places using stepped foundations. This section is easily accessible by car. From Carvoran the farm road to Walltown provides a good area for parking and a footpath sign directs one up to the Wall. Sadly, this excellent section is brought to an abrupt end by the western end of the Walltown quarry which has removed the rest of the Nine Nicks of Thirlwell and the Wall with them. To the modern mind this savage intrusion of industry upon our national historical heritage seems to be nothing less than sheer vandalism.

It is pleasing to note that there are plans to reclaim this area of desolation. Whinstone was quarried at Walltown Quarry until 1978 and, in addition to removing the Wall, the quarry working left a 40 acre hole up to 100 feet deep, flooded in parts and littered by derelict buildings and mineral waste. The quarry area has now been bought by Northumberland County Council who are carrying out a major environmental improvement scheme. The material from the construction of the Greenhead By-pass is being used to raise the floor of the quarry and to provide drainage to prevent flooding, and the area will be grassed and parts of the site planted with young trees. It is hoped to develop the whole area as an historical and archaeological theme park based on the history of the Roman Wall and of Roman Britain in general. One possibility being considered is the reconstruction of a section of the Wall along its original line and to its original size. It would seem highly fitting that the Wall should be recreated in the very spot where it was totally destroyed, and if there is anywhere that a huge reconstruction should be built, nowhere would seem more appropriate than in the area of desolation created by Walltown Quarry.

Just west of the quarry lies the Roman fort of Carvoran and the Carvoran Roman Army Museum. The fort lies on the Stanegate about 130 yards south of the Wall and, like Vindolanda, was originally part of the pre-Hadrianic frontier. Its purpose was to safeguard the junction of the Stanegate with the Maiden Way, the Roman road running south to Kirkby Thore, and also to guard the valley of the Tipalt Burn. Substantial remains of the fort survived until the 18th century when the ruins were levelled for agricultural purposes and only one angle turret can now be seen. The site is owned by the Vindolanda Trust, and will no doubt be fully excavated at some time in the future.

The Roman Army Museum, which is run by the Trust, is based upon the old farmhouse of Carvoran and houses an excellent collection of exhibits. It is a spacious museum with displays of many Roman objects, and also of several reconstructions, models and life-size figures. There is a film theatre, coffee shop and bookshop, where an informative teacher's pack may be purchased.

The central display in the hall is of a lifesize model of a cavalry officer standing beside his horse, which is a sturdy animal 14 hands high. The officer wears a mail tunic over warm underclothes and carries a long spear, a sword and a shield. The horse's saddle is based on the remains of one found at Vindolanda in 1987. For most of the Roman occupation of Britain there were 14 cavalry regiments in the province.

There is also an excellent model of the fort at Carvoran with a stretch of Wall to the north, including Milecastle 46. The model is on a huge scale and is illuminated at the touch of a button. A commentary describes the various features of the fort. This is a very good way to present the layout of a Roman fort and to indicate the nature of its internal buildings. Serious students would do well to view this model before visiting the other forts on the Wall. Other models on display include a fort granary, a headquarters building and a milecastle. There is a replica of an ox-wagon and also a fine display of armour and equipment.

Among larger displays there is a lifelike reconstruction of the inside of a barrack block. A soldier is shown sitting on one of two double bunks and the window contains the pale green glass used by the Romans. In an audio-visual display a legionary soldier explains that he has come from Chester to check on supplies before the troops start on the construction of the Wall.

The Museum conveys much information about life in the Roman army. Food was an important issue to soldiers and they ate well. Fresh vegetables were appreciated when available and they also enjoyed fish as a change from meat dishes. Oysters were popular and could be obtained from oyster beds at South Shields. Meat was often highly spiced to disguise the taste after being stored during the winter! Soldiers were also talented craftsmen and many of their tools and iron fittings are displayed. Much information is provided about the Roman occupation of Britain and there is a list of the forts on Hadrian's Wall with photographs and details of what to see at each site.

# CHAPTER 7

## *Carvoran to Carlisle*

Walltown Crags mark the end of the high country of the Whin Sill. Ahead lie the rolling pastoral plains of Cumbria leading to the shores of the Solway Firth. But although we are now leaving what is traditionally regarded as Wall country there are still significant remains of the Wall frontier to be seen.

From the Roman Army Museum head north along the road to Low Tipalt for about 40 yards before taking a footpath left which is signposted as the Pennine Way. The path runs along the north side of the Ditch which is very prominent here as it descends to the Tipalt Burn. The unexpected sight of a train ahead reminds one of the proximity of the Newcastle to Carlisle line, which runs just to the west of the village of Greenhead. But unfortunately there is no station in the village, the nearest being at Haltwhistle, over three miles away to the south-east. The ruins of Thirlwall Castle, a 14th century peel tower built of stones taken from the Wall, lie high on a grassy mound to the north. Its rather grim exterior reminds one of the harsh realities of life in the border country. The path crosses the Tipalt Burn by a footbridge just beside Holmhead Guest House. Refreshments may be obtained here and hikers are said to be welcome.

After crossing the burn the path follows the Pennine Way across the railway and rejoins the familiar B6318. The village of Greenhead lies half a mile to the south, but our route lies north-west for a quarter of a mile along the road before we turn left on to the line of the Wall on a path signposted to Chapel House. Just before the footpath sign there is a short section of Wall preserved on the grass bank on the right of the road. The Ditch is in excellent condition here and the route is well signposted throughout this stretch. Although one may have to pass the occasional bull, they seem fairly docile in these parts! The path crosses a farm road and continues ahead over pleasant, grassy pastures to the farm of Gap. After passing through the farm one continues across two roads to enter the outskirts of Gilsland.

A narrow pathway beside the railway leads to Milecastle 48 (Poltross Burn) which lies on a steep slope on the western side of the burn and is in very fine condition. Its walls extending about 12 feet on either side were built to the Broad gauge. One should note a series of ovens built into the north-west angle and the remains of a flight of steps in its north-east corner from which it has been calculated that the external level of the rampart walk was 15 feet high. Traces of a pair of barrack blocks show that these originally consisted of four rooms each and could have accommodated a garrison of 64 men, thought to be the largest possible in any milecastle. The visitor today is left to wonder how its inhabitants overcame the steepness of the slope in planning their sleeping arrangements!

On leaving the milecastle one should take the footpath that runs beside the railway, which is signposted to Willowford Roman Wall. A yellow arrow indicates where the railway may be crossed, and as one descends the embankment one has a good view of a long stretch of well preserved Wall which runs through the rather unkempt gardens of the old vicarage. A gate on the Brampton road provides access to this section. After crossing the road there is a very fine continuous stretch of Narrow Wall built on Broad foundation, which runs for just over half a mile down to the River Irthing. The Wall rises to ten courses in places and this section includes Turret 48a which has fine wing walls of Broad gauge. There are also clear traces of the Ditch.

The final stretch down to the Roman bridge is on private land and one should visit Willowford Farm to pay the small fee required. A centurial stone together with a translation has recently been placed in the north wall of a barn just beside the entrance to the farmyard. On my last visit I met the farmer who said that visitors came from all over the world. Some of them were just as keen to watch him lambing or calving as to see the Wall. He said that people left very little litter, but for security they always had to make sure that someone was about on the farm. Reflecting on the skill of the Romans in constructing the bridge, he commented: 'They were as clever in them days as we are today!'

From the farm the Wall descends a grassy slope to reach

The Wall running down to the River Irthing at Willowford. This is
Narrow Wall on a Broad foundation.

the abutment of the bridge which took it over the Irthing. The river has changed its course considerably since Roman times and now flows much further to the west. The remains are difficult to understand, because there are probably traces of three bridges on the site. The first bridge abutment was guarded by a small turret at the end of the Wall. When the second bridge was built, the Wall was extended westwards and the original turret was replaced by a larger one placed a few feet to the east. Two narrow culverts at the end of the Wall probably served as a water-mill. Finally, in its third phase, the bridge was enlarged to carry the Military Way across. Part of the old mill-race was filled in and replaced by a larger one and the abutment was increased in size. Traces of one pier of this bridge may be seen, west of the enlarged abutment.

Those who come equipped with wellingtons and a stout stick may attempt to follow in the steps of the Romans and ford the river at this point. Although fast running, the river is not deep and there are no particular problems. A path winds steeply up the cliff to Harrow's Scar, where a fine section of Wall leads straight to Birdoswald Fort. The steepness of the cliff nowadays is due to the change in the river bed. In Roman times the climb was more gradual.

Timorous mortals must return to the village to cross the Irthing at the Bridge Inn and then turn left to continue on the B6318. A seat placed by the roadside provides a good view of the Irthing gorge and of the Wall sweeping down to the river and resuming on the cliff top to the fort at Birdoswald. A footpath left provides a short cut through a small wood across to the car park at Birdoswald. There is a stream at the bottom of the wood where in early summer primroses and bluebells provide an idyllic pastoral setting. I once disturbed a deer here.

From the cliff top at Harrow's Scar there is a fine view through the trees of the Willowford bridge abutment and the Wall snaking up the slope towards the farm. Immediately above the edge of the cliff there are the well-preserved remains of Milecastle 49 (Harrow's Scar). The stone which remains visible today replaced an earlier milecastle built of turf and timber. The south gate was considerably altered in the later

Roman period and the tombstone of a two year old boy
was found reused in the foundations. Within the milecastle
the remains of a post-medieval farmhouse may be seen.

West of the River Irthing the Wall was originally built of turf
and in this stretch it ran slightly to the south of the stone
Wall which replaced it towards the end of the 120s AD. A
very good stretch of stone Wall runs westwards for a third
of a mile from Harrow Scar Milecastle to Birdoswald fort.
This stretch contains in its south face a number of centurial
stones, marking lengths built by different legionary working
parties. These stones are often difficult to spot but one may
clearly be seen in the ninth and highest surviving course of the
Wall just 20 yards to the east of a very marshy section where the
path has to make a detour. The markings COH VIII JUL PRIM
may easily be picked out, indicating that this section was built
by the Eighth Cohort of Julius Primus.

The fort of Birdoswald should be entered by the new visitor
centre at the old farmhouse, which occupies the north-west
corner of the fort. The site was farmed until 1984 when it
was acquired by Cumbria County Council who have recently
conducted an extensive series of excavations. An altar which
records the Roman name of the fort as Banna is now in the
undercroft at Lanercost Priory. An excellent leaflet is provided
describing the main features of the site, although one has to
remember that it predates the current excavations.

Although the headquarters building and most of the other
internal buildings are under grass, almost all the fort wall
surrounding the southern part of the fort is visible. Some fine
ovens may be seen built into the back of the rampart bank by
the south gate. It was near here in 1949 that a soldier's purse
was found under the rampart. This contained his pay and had
been lost at the time when the fort was being constructed. The
east gate is one of the best preserved on the Wall, surviving at
its southern end to the base of the arch. Like all main gateways it
originally consisted of two passageways flanked by guardrooms
on either side. Its northern passageway was later blocked to
restrict movement.

Excavations between 1987–90 uncovered the remains of a
pair of granaries. An inscription found in 1929 tells us that
they were built between AD 205-208 by Aurelius Julianus, the

Ovens built into the rampart of the south gate of Birdoswald.

commander of the unit of Dacians, soldiers recruited in what is now Romania, who formed the fort garrison. This same Julianus buried his infant son in the cemetery of the civil settlement which grew up outside the fort. The inscription he put up was later reused as paving on one of the barrack blocks. It reads: 'To the spirits of the departed and of Aurelius Concordius: he lived one year five days, son of Aurelius Julianus, the tribune.'

Granaries were long, narrow buildings with buttressed walls. The floors were raised above ground level, and slots were pierced through the walls below the floors to allow ventilation. At Birdoswald these features have survived better than anywhere else on the Wall. The granaries were built into the side of a slope and were buttressed only on the southern, downhill side. Buttresses were needed to support the weight of stored grain, and also of the heavy stone roof. In the south granary double entrances were provided at each end and the pivot holes which held uprights for wooden doors to swing on are clearly visible. There was also a small entrance to the space under the

The recently excavated south granary at Birdoswald.

floor, which was probably designed to allow dogs to clear the rats and other pests.

Excavations have now started on the west gate. This seems to have survived for many years and to have continued in use in the early Middle Ages. The excavators have uncovered a great deal of information about the history of the site in the post-Roman period. Medieval farmers built houses and barns inside the fort walls for protection and during the period of border raids it seems that a peel tower was built here. When in 1599 Reginald Bainbrigg visited the Wall he went to Birdoswald which, he wrote, 'doth seame to have been some great towne by the great ruynes thereof.' The present farmhouse dates from the late 16th century and was enlarged in 1745. A watercolour painting of Birdoswald fort completed in 1848 by Henry Richardson shows that by then the original house had been transformed into a peaceful farm. In the 1850s it was owned by Henry Norman, a Victorian romantic who extended it further and built the mock peel tower which we see today. He also laid out an ornamental garden, using the south wall of the Roman south granary as a ha-ha to prevent sheep gaining access.

The north-west corner of the fort wall at Birdoswald with the 19th century mock peel tower behind.

Birdoswald is located at one of the most picturesque settings along the whole of the Wall. Cattle and sheep graze beside the fort and it is a delight to stroll round its walls. One should also walk southwards to the edge of the fort platform to see the spectacular view south-west of the Irthing Gorge. There is a fine museum which contains a great deal of information about the fort, the later history of the site and the recent excavations. There is also a small shop and a picnic area. In a small film theatre a 25 minute BBC film is shown at regular intervals, telling the imaginative story of how a boy and girl from Brampton School meet the son and daughter of the fort commander, Aurelius Julianus. It also includes an interview with Tony Wilmot, who was director of the recent excavations.

On leaving the fort one should notice its rounded north-west corner which rises to 13 courses in places. As one proceeds westwards there is a fine stretch of Wall for over 400 yards, at the far end of which may be seen the low remains of Turret 49b. The Ditch becomes prominent on the right of the road and the Vallum can be seen across the field on the left. Just over a mile west of Birdoswald, immediately opposite Appletree barn, one should turn left for 100 yards to view a section of the Turf Wall. For a short distance west of Birdoswald this followed a different route from the stone Wall which replaced it. The Turf Wall is visible as a broad grassy mound at the side of the farm road, about 30 yards north of the Vallum, whose mounds and ditch are very well preserved in this section. Clear signs of the Turf Wall ditch may be seen on its northern side.

Half a mile further on the well preserved remains of Turret 51a (Piper Sike) may be seen on the right of the road. There is a stone platform, possibly for a ladder, against its north wall and a sunken hearth may also be seen. A few feet of curtain Wall survive to the west. Just after passing the lane to Gunshaw Farm one comes upon Turret 51b (Leahill). This is also very well preserved with a short section of curtain wall to the west. It seems that it was mainly used in the second century.

Pike Hill signal tower lies on the left of the road just west of the village of Bank. It occupies the highest point in the area and has very fine views in all directions. This tower was built before the construction of the Wall and seems to have been a signalling tower. It lies at a 45 degree angle to the line of the Wall and has deep foundations, which suggests it may have been higher than a normal turret. It was obviously regarded as an important feature because it was retained in use when the Wall was built despite the nearby presence of Banks Turret. Much of its northern area was destroyed in 1870 when the road was lowered to its present position.

200 yards further east lie the fine remains of Turret 52a (Banks East). Its walls rise to 10 courses high in places and there are 20 yards or more of curtain Wall on either side of it. It commands a fine view southwards over the valley of the Irthing, and westwards to the Lakeland hills, with Skiddaw and Blencathra dominating the skyline. Note the straight joint between the turret and the curtain wall on both sides, which shows that the turret was here before the Turf Wall was rebuilt in stone. This turret was in use from the Hadrianic period until the end of the third century. Banks Turret and Pike Hill Signal

Lanercost Priory and gatehouse.

Tower are linked by a gravel footpath and there is a small car-park between the two sites.

One mile south-west of Banks lie the 12th century ruins of Lanercost Priory. The priory has a lovely setting on a low plain by the River Irthing. It is entered through a ruined arch, which is all that remains of the original priory gatehouse. As one approaches the church one passes the Vicarage, whose eastern end was the 13th century guest-house. This priory of Augustinian Canons was founded in 1166 by Robert de Vaux, the Norman lord of Gilsland and is dedicated to St Mary Magdalene. A statue of her may be seen high up on the exterior west wall and beside her is the kneeling half-sized figure of a Canon. The priory was largely constructed of stones taken from the Roman Wall and two inscribed stones may still be seen. One bearing an inscription of the Sixth Legion has been placed upside down high up on the north wall of the vicarage. The other, a centurial inscription, is in the north wall of the cloisters immediately above the right hand end of an open doorway, which is at present used to store a wheelbarrow.

One famous possession of the priory was the Lanercost Cartulary. Grants of land to the priory were recorded on slips of parchment called charters, the equivalent of title deeds today. Some time between 1252 and 1256 the Canons had their charters copied into a book for ready reference. This Cartulary was continued up to 1364 and was later illustrated with sketches and coats of arms. The book disappeared after 1826 and was not rediscovered until 1982. Another ancient relic of the past is the Lanercost Cross. The base of this cross lies on the green outside the church. The upper part stands in the north-west corner of the nave. Originally it bore an inscription recording the fact that it was made in the year 1214. In 1657 it was reused rather pathetically as the tombstone for the grave of a little boy who died at the age of two.

Lanercost suffered heavily in the Border Wars. The cloisters were burnt in 1296 and in the following year the priory was attacked by William Wallace. Edward I, who conducted ruthless campaigns against the Scots, came to Lanercost three times. He made his last visit in September 1306. He only intended to stay a few days but his health was poor and he was obliged to remain at the guesthouse of the Priory until the following spring. The Great Seal was brought here, and during the winter Lanercost became the centre of English government. In March 1307 Edward left to hold a Parliament at Carlisle and died shortly afterwards at Burgh-by-Sands on the banks of the Solway. In 1311 Robert Bruce came to Lanercost and imprisoned most of the canons as punishment for the hospitality they had given to Edward.

When the Priories were dissolved by Henry VIII in 1536 the canons were turned out of Lanercost and all valuables were confiscated. Lead, timber and stone were carried away, and the building was left as a ruin. A tiny church was retained in the north aisle, and in the 18th century the nave was reroofed and separated from the remainder of the church by a wall. In the 19th century the church was beautified by the Earl of Carlisle's family who were patrons of the pre-Raphaelite artists. There is a Burne-Jones memorial to Charles Howard the 5th son of the Earl of Carlisle and several William Morris windows in the priory. Apart from three small fragments, the east window contains no stained glass and provides a clear view of the priory ruins from the church. Placed in a riverside setting and surrounded by meadows, Lanercost Priory occupies a delightful position. It has been a centre of worship for over 800 years and serves today as the active parish church for a small and scattered rural community. Excellent views may be had of the priory from the riverside footpath and time should be taken to savour its surroundings. There is also a fine selection of home-made marmalade usually available, on sale in aid of church funds.

From Banks one should make an excursion to the outpost fort of Bewcastle, which lies 7½ miles to the north and is well sign-posted from the village. The fort is situated in a remote and lonely setting on a high plateau above the swift-flowing Kirk Beck. It was unusual in being six-sided to make the best use of the six acre site. Traces of the ramparts and ditches can be seen and within the central area lie the church, the castle and the old rectory. The fort was built at the same time as the Wall and was directly linked to Birdoswald by the Roman road known as the Maiden Way. Although the present church only dates back to 1792, the site has been a place of Christian worship for more than 1000 years.

In the churchyard there is the famous Bewcastle Cross, one of the most impressive monuments to survive from the days of early Christianity in northern England. It is made of yellow sandstone and stands 14½ feet high. It is thought to date from the late seventh or early eighth century AD. A stone barn at the south of the churchyard contains a permanent exhibition entitled 'Bewcastle past and present'. The centrepiece is a brightly coloured mural illustrating Bewcastle through the ages. It depicts a Roman soldier, a Saxon settlement, the Bewcastle Cross, stonework from the Norman castle, a shepherd, low flying aircraft, Galloway cattle and Scottish Black-Faced sheep. The cross is shown as it might have looked when first erected. A leaflet is available from the nearby farm giving details of the castle. This was constructed in the north-east corner of the fort, which provided a good defensive position and excellent building materials.

Bewcastle lies in a remote moorland setting and in the 16th century played its full part in border warfare. Local legend has

The Bewcastle Cross.

it that at one time only the women were buried there — the men were hanged at Carlisle! A visit to the site may suitably be concluded at the Limekiln Inn, which lies in a hollow below the church. Here by a blazing log fire one may enjoy the unspoilt atmosphere of a genuine local inn.

After returning to Banks one should head westwards by a footpath signposted to the village of Walton. This leads up to an interesting stretch of the Wall at Hare Hill. This section about nine feet high is often said to be the highest surviving fragment of Hadrian's Wall but in fact it was substantially rebuilt in the 19th century. Only the bottom two courses of stone work are Roman masonry in its original position. But all the stones must originally have come from the Wall, and one of the north facing stones bears an inscription PP, signifying that it once marked a stretch of Wall built or rebuilt by the century of men under the primus pilus (the chief centurion of a legion).

After passing through a farm, traces of the Ditch appear on the right. The path continues ahead due west, passing over a succession of stiles. In the bed of the Ditch buttercups grow in profusion in early summer and the white blossom of the blackthorn is impressive. As one begins the descent of Hare Hill there are extensive views westward towards the sea, and, to the south west the northern mountains of the Lake District may be clearly seen. The field wall on the right is built on the grass-covered Wall foundation, which is occasionally visible through the grass. As we approach Haytongate Farm the Ditch becomes very impressive with trees growing on either side of it. After crossing the farm road the path continues westwards and the Wall is seen as a vague hump beneath the hedge on one's right, with the occasional stone visible. This is pleasant walking along a broad grassy path across a meadow down to a stream. The path is easy to follow and there are definite traces of rough, unconserved Wall three or four feet high in places, covered in grass with a hedge growing on top.

After passing the farm of Garthside one emerges on to a tarmac road where one should turn right and then left to follow the road for two miles to the village of Walton. I attempted to keep to the line of the Wall but got into considerable difficulties. I had to climb three barbed wire fences before

The Wall at Hare Hill. This section about nine feet high was rebuilt in the 19th century.

giving up. I also found that traces of the Wall system were very indistinct. After this experience I was slightly mollified to read in the *Handbook* that 'the Wall now becomes difficult to follow through the arable fields'.

On approaching the village of Walton the road drops steeply to cross the King Water at Dovecot Bridge. Just after crossing the bridge a Wall notice directs one through a small field gate on the right, where there is a short but impressive length of grass-covered Wall about ten yards long. An English Heritage notice states that in 1983 this stretch of Wall, which was the only visible part built of Cumbrian red sandstone, was clamped in earth and reburied. It had been exposed for nearly 20 years and in that time the weather had seriously damaged the stones. There are two photos on the site, which show the Wall just before it was back-filled and reveal the state of the erosion.

The village of Walton is a peaceful spot with a delightful village green. The church is built of mellowed red Cumbrian sandstone, and there is a sober red-brick village school marked out by a clock. The inn is aptly named the Centurion Inn and apparently lies directly over the course of the Wall. I had an excellent late lunch of Cumberland sausage here and enjoyed the company of some Cumbrian folk.

After leaving the inn one turns right on to an obvious path which brings one past the back of Sandysike, an attractive house with a fine walled garden. After passing through the farmyard one should turn left through a gate into a field and continue ahead down to the Cam Beck. There are a few signs here of the Wall Ditch. A quarter of a mile to the south lie the ruins of the Roman fort of Castlesteads. There is some doubt over its Roman name but it is thought to be Camboglanna. It was not placed on the line of the Wall, which had already been built, but was positioned on a high platform commanding the Cam Beck valley, guarding an important line of approach to the Wall. The site was drastically levelled in 1791 when the gardens of Castlesteads House were laid over it and its north-west front has been eroded by the Cam Beck. There are few remains visible today.

The crossing of the weir at Cam Beck requires a certain dexterity if one is to remain dry. The water is shallow at the top but the crossing is narrow and there is a steep drop to the left. Considering discretion the better part of valour I walked in the bed of the stream rather than at the edge of the weir and got wet feet in the process. After crossing the stream the path continues south-west to the farm of Cambeckhill. After crossing the farm road one should continue ahead through a field and over a small stream to the aptly named The Beck Farm, which is built of mellow Cumbrian red sandstone. This stretch is well signposted with yellow arrows indicating the line of the footpath. The path continues past Head's Wood and over a series of stiles to the village of Newtown.

Newtown is a quiet little hamlet on the A6071 Brampton to Longton road. The route lies straight ahead down the lane leading to Irthington, and where the road turns south, one should go straight ahead along a footpath signposted Old Wall. Continue over stiles and across a large field with a flooded ditch at its side, keeping the hedge and fence always on the right and heading directly south-west. Do not deviate right on to the clearly defined path for Laversdale. On reaching the farm buildings of Old Wall one has a good view of Carlisle Airport.

One should continue ahead on the same line encouraged by a footpath optimistically signposted 'Roman Wall'. Apart from a few traces of the Ditch and some grass-covered mounds there have been no obvious signs of the Wall system for some distance. Stiles and gates lead through fields and down a lane past Bleatarn and across a common to Wall Head Farm where one joins the tarmac road running from Highfieldmoor.

This is a pleasant country lane, straight and narrow with high hedges on either side. Some traces now appear of the Ditch on the right. The road runs straight for two miles, presumably built on the Wall itself. One can hear the distant hum of the M6 motorway accompanied by the droning of planes from Carlisle Airport, but occasionally the plaintive cry of the curlew can also be heard. Where the road swings left it is possible to continue ahead down a farm road and on to a section of ditch, but there are problems crossing fences and considerable persistence is required. The easier course is to follow the lane round to join the B6264 Brampton to Carlisle road.

This leads across the motorway and straight into Carlisle. Some consolation for the absence of the Wall is provided by the housing estates Hadrian's Park and Centurion's Walk, both of which are built very near to the line of the Wall. Any Wall pilgrims who have walked from Newcastle will be encouraged to read the notice of welcome provided by Carlisle City Council and will no doubt do their best to live up to the City motto 'Be just and fear not.' For weary feet it is quite a long trek down into the city, although it is reassuring to catch glimpses of the Eden Bridge and the Castle through the trees ahead.

Just to the north of the bridge lies the suburb of Stanwix and one's route into Carlisle brings one past the southern end of Stanwix churchyard. The Roman fort at Stanwix lay on the fine natural platform now occupied by the church and the mound of the south rampart has been traced in the churchyard. The fort was sited here to guard the Eden bridge and to control the western route to Scotland. The fort area covered some nine acres, and was intended for the Ala Petriana from Gaul, the only cavalry regiment 1000 strong on the Wall and the senior auxiliary regiment of the army in Britain. The fort was named Petriana after its garrison. It is clear that Stanwix was the most important position on the Wall and the seat of the senior commanding officer.

Before the construction of the fort of Stanwix there was a Roman fort at Carlisle south of the Eden beside the River Caldew. When the Wall was constructed and the garrison transferred to Stanwix, Carlisle became the city of Luguvalium. It seems to have developed into an extensive town of about 74 acres and was the capital of the local tribe, the Carvetii. Its walls were still an impressive site when St Cuthbert paid a visit here in AD 685. The numerous Roman finds which have been made in the city are now housed in the Tullie House Museum. The Roman bridge over the Eden lay to the north of the present cricket ground. When William Camden came here in 1599 he recorded seeing mighty stones within the channel of the river. When the river was dredged in 1951 many stones were recovered from its bed, including one slab inscribed by the century of Vesnius Viator. These stones have been laid out in a small enclosure beside the river in Bitts Park.

# CHAPTER 8

## *Carlisle to Bowness on Solway*

In the early days of the Roman occupation of Britain Carlisle served as a major military base, and after the building of Hadrian's Wall it became the most important civilian settlement on the northern frontier of the Roman empire. Conquest by Vikings, Angles and Saxons followed and at the time when the Domesday book was being compiled the city was actually part of Scotland and so was not included! For several centuries Carlisle was the scene of bitter fighting as the line of the England-Scotland border fluctuated north and south of it. The establishment of a united kingdom under James I did not end the city's experience of warfare. During the Civil War Carlisle took the royalist side and after the siege of 1644–45 it was captured by the Scots. It surrendered to the Scots again in 1745 when Bonnie Prince Charlie staked his claim to the English throne by declaring his father king from the steps of Carlisle Cross. The last time its guns were fired in anger was in 1746 when it was retaken by the Duke of Cumberland as he made his way to the battle of Culloden. The city's 1700 years of strife are surely unique in the annals of any English town. It is not for nothing that the city has a Scots Street, leading into the main square from the north, and an English Street leading out of it to the south. I suppose that was one way of hedging their bets.

In the last 200 years Carlisle has developed into the regional capital of Cumbria and the Borders. Some of the stores in the central square have a drab and rather dated appearance but the city's ability to blend its ancient history with new development is typified by the opening in 1984 of The Lanes shopping precinct, which was voted the best new large shopping centre in Britain. The fountain depicting otters playing in the water creates a relaxed atmosphere, and children seem to enjoy playing there as much as the otters do. This air of relaxation is enhanced by the unusual statue of Jimmy Dyer, well known locally as an itinerant fiddler and ballad singer.

Carlisle Cathedral is one of the smallest in England. It began life as an Augustinian priory and became the cathedral church in 1133 when the Diocese of Carlisle was founded. It was built largely of stones from the Roman Wall. After the capture of the city in 1645 Scottish troops under General Leslie used many of the stones from the nave and the monastic buildings to repair the city walls and the castle. About two thirds of the nave was destroyed at this time, so that now only about 39 feet remain of the original 140 feet of the nave built by the Normans. There is a fine Early English choir of about 1225 and some excellent examples of 15th and 16th century wood carving, including a misericord which depicts a mermaid. A prized treasure is the Brougham Triptych, a magnificent 16th century carved Flemish altarpiece. The cathedral's crowning glory, however, is its Decorated east window, which is one of the finest in Europe. It measures 51 feet high and 26 feet wide, and retains original 14th century glass in its tracery.

Sir Walter Scott was married here in 1797. The house in Castle Street where he was staying is marked by a plaque. Among many memorials to local people there are tablets commemorating Canon Frederick Rawnsley (1851–1928), the founder of the National Trust, and the Revd Theodore Hardy VC DSO MC, who died in 1918 and was the most decorated non-combatant in the 1st World War. The cathedral has the unusual record of having had only ten organists in the past 330 years. Andrew Sievewright who retired in 1991 as cathedral organist managed to put in a mere 30 years! In the cloister there is the fratry, a fine 14th century refectory which is still in use as a library; there is an excellent buttery in the undercroft. Also within the cathedral precincts lies the Deanery. This was originally the prior's lodging and part of the building is a 16th century peel tower.

Beside the cathedral lies the church of St Cuthbert. The present building was constructed in 1778 but there has been a church on this site for many centuries. The church is in regular use and is kept in beautiful condition. The interior is Georgian and a pleasingly light effect is created by its blue carpet and white pillars. An unusual feature is a moveable pulpit which runs on railway lines and may be pushed to one side when not in use. Another distinctive feature is a Latvian window

The fratry, Carlisle Cathedral.

bearing the coat of arms of Latvia together with a map showing the position of the capital Riga. This window was the gift of Latvians who fled to Britain after the Second World War and especially of those who worshipped in this church. Alongside the church there is a 15th century tithe barn which was restored in 1971 and further to the west there are extensive remains of the medieval city wall.

Carlisle castle was built in 1092 and enlarged in the 12th century mainly with stones taken from Hadrian's Wall. For over 600 years it played a leading role in the bitter fighting of the border area. Edward I held his last parliament here in 1307 and Mary Queen of Scots began her imprisonment here in 1568. Between 1827 and 1835 much of the building was pulled down, including the great hall and tower. It is now in the care of English Heritage and the keep houses the fine museum of the Border Regiment.

Any visitor who arrives at Carlisle by train is confronted on leaving the station by the twin towers of the citadel. These were erected in 1810 from designs by Thomas Telford. They

Carlisle Castle.

replaced similar structures built by Henry VIII in 1542. They were originally joined by a curtain wall and their purpose was to guard the southern approach to the city and to serve as an additional defence to the castle.

The Guildhall is an interesting medieval half-timbered building. It was built as a town house about 1400 and was later used as a meeting place for Carlisle's eight medieval trade guilds. It was extensively renovated in 1978 and is now a Museum of Guild, Civic and Local History.

Carlisle has a large and attractive main square which is now a traffic-free precinct. The Tourist Information Centre is housed in the 18th century town hall, in front of which is the market cross which dates back to 1682. Beside the cross is a replica Victorian pillar box, which was installed in 1989 to commemorate the fact that in 1853 Carlisle was the first place in mainland Britain to have a roadside pillar box.

No Wall pilgrim can visit Carlisle without calling at Tullie House. This is the museum where finds from the civil settlement and from neighbouring forts on the Wall have been deposited. The original house was built in 1689 and enlarged at the end of

The 17th century Carel Cross in the market place, Carlisle.

the last century. In the garden one may go down some steps to see the foundation of a 3rd century native shrine. The Museum has recently undergone a multi-million pound development and now uses the latest techniques to recreate the experiences of Carlisle's long history. It is now possible to stroll through Roman Carlisle, climb stairs forming part of the Turf Wall, come face to face with a Border Reiver, or sit in the 3rd class compartment of a railway carriage. A lecture theatre provides a varied programme of films, videos and lectures. There is a well-stocked bookshop and a comfortable cafe. A visit to Tullie House is a powerful experience, but opinions may vary as to its lasting effectiveness. One cannot help feeling that the prime motive of the organisers is to dispel boredom rather than to banish ignorance.

Two of the outpost forts north of the Wall may conveniently be visited from Carlisle. Netherby is situated overlooking the River Esk six miles north-east of Gretna. In Roman times it was a port, but the coastline has receded considerably since then and it is now several miles from the sea. Unfortunately there is nothing for the modern visitor to see. The site is on private property on the Netherby Estate and all traces of the fort were destroyed in the early 18th century when improvements were made to Netherby Castle.

Birrens lies 20 miles north-west of Carlisle. One should leave the A74 seven miles north-west of Gretna by a minor road leading to the village of Middlebie. The grass-covered ramparts of the fort lie on the right of the road just before entering the village. The ruins may be approached through a gate opposite a white-washed cottage with the appropriate name Birrens Cottage. The ramparts survive as bold mounds on the east, north and west, but the southern portion of the fort has been washed away by the Mein Water.

After returning to Carlisle the final stage of the journey to Bowness-on-Solway starts from the bridge over the Eden. After crossing the river the Wall ran through what is now the city's sewage disposal works and cannot be followed directly! From the bridge one should walk through the beautiful Bitts Park, keeping close to the river and passing to the north of the Castle. Just before crossing the tributary River Caldew one passes a small enclosure which contains the stones from the

Roman bridge over the Eden which were found in the river
bed in 1951. After crossing the Caldew, one should swing right
beside the sports ground and follow the riverside path along
the Eden. Cattle grazing by the river and in the river bed
itself create a pleasing pastoral scene. One may now follow
signs for the Cumbria Coastal Way, a recently created long
distance walk. As one passes the strangely named Knockupworth
Farm, traces appear of the Vallum, the first remainder of the
Wall system since leaving Carlisle. In summer bluebells and
forget-me-nots create a vivid expanse of colour in a peaceful
and pastoral scene. The path provides good walking and is well
signposted throughout.

The small church at Grinsdale is situated on a grassy knoll
overlooking the River Eden at the eastern end of the village.
There is no sign indicating the presence of the church and
without a map you would not even know of its existence. It is
approached by a grassy lane and lies in a peaceful spot above
the river. Sheep and horses graze in a field below and a fringe
of trees provides shelter on the south and east. Unfortunately
the church was locked when I visited it, but I could see its simple
interior through a window on the north side. It is dedicated
to St Kentigern and was built in 1740. The riverside setting
of Grinsdale Church is one of the most beautiful sites of any
church in England. It was such a peaceful spot in the afternoon
sun that I was reluctant to leave.

From the village one should take the signposted footpath
through Park Farm and along a broad grassy track to the
village of Kirkandrews-on-Eden. Here one should join the
Beaumont road and after 200 yards turn right on to a public
footpath which leads down to the river bank. The river is very
slow-moving here and all is serene and quiet. One cannot
help reflecting that the Wall must have seemed a fierce and
unwelcome intrusion into this peaceful and placid countryside.
After passing over a footbridge the path climbs to join the road
leading into the village of Beaumont.

There is an attractive village green beside the church. A
modern seat surrounding a tree in the centre commemorates
the visit of the Mayor of Carlisle in April 1991. St Mary's
Church was built of red sandstone taken from the Roman Wall
and has several ancient features. The east window is 12th

St Kentigern's Church, Grindsdale.

century although its glass is Victorian, and the timber roof dates back to the 15th century. The porch is 19th century and incorporates a reused Norman arch. The church has a white-washed interior and boasts a list of rectors back to 1296. From the churchyard there is a clear view north-west across the Solway Firth.

One leaves the village by turning left down a gravel lane which runs along the line of the Wall. To the south there are good views of the Lakeland hills dominated by Skiddaw. There seem to be some traces of the Wall foundations in the roots of trees on one's left. The path, which is clearly marked out by a line of trees, passes over a stile and footbridge to join the road leading to the village of Burgh-by-Sands, where lay the Roman fort of Aballava.

Very little is known of the fort at Burgh-by-Sands. Only its eastern wall has been located for certain, but its size has been calculated at about 5 acres. Its function was to guard the southern end of two important fords across the Solway. St Michael's Church lies within the area of the fort and is built

The 14th century tower, St Michael's Church, Burgh-by-Sands.

The Edward I monument on Burgh Marsh.

almost entirely of Roman stones. It has a wonderfully rugged exterior and is a fine specimen of a fortified Border church. Its low 14th century tower has small windows and no exterior door and was built with a mind to defence against the Scots. Its walls are seven feet thick and there is an iron grill shutting it off from the nave. At the eastern end of the church there is a fortified house for the vicar apparently built in the late medieval period; the base is now used as a vestry. The main entrance to the church is through the remains of a Norman arch and a farmyard abuts the churchyard on the south side. The age-old peaceful atmosphere of the village was typified for me on a hot summer's day by a procession of cows passing through at a leisurely pace, with the cowman on a bicycle behind them.

Two miles north of the village lies Burgh Marsh, where Edward I encamped in 1307, waiting for a favourable opportunity to cross the Solway and attack the Scots. He died, however, on 7th July that year and in 1685 a large monument was erected on the spot where local tradition placed his tent. It was restored in 1876 by the Earl of Lonsdale. It stands

today on the grassy marsh-flats, brooding over the Solway
in lonely isolation, surrounded only by the grazing cattle. Its
lonely splendour creates a strange, melancholy atmosphere.
One leaves the village by the Drumburgh road, which runs
along the edge of the marsh. There are warning notices of the
dangers of bathing and venturing out over the sands at low tide,
and there are frequent reminders that the road is liable to tidal
flooding. After passing the hamlet of Dykesfield it is possible to
walk on the high grass bank of the old canal, later used as the
embankment for the disused railway. There are black and white
poles on each side of the road, presumably to act as markers
during flooding.

Just before entering Drumburgh the grass-covered railway
bank swings north to follow the line of the coast, but one should
keep with the road to pass through the village. The Roman
fort of Drumburgh occupied a bold platform just to the west
of the village and was very small, occupying less than 2 acres.
There appear to be no visible signs today. Drumburgh Castle
lies on the south side of the village street. This is a fine 16th
century Cumbrian manor house, built almost entirely out of red
sandstone taken from the Wall. The antiquary, John Leland,
chaplain and librarian to Henry VIII, noted that: 'The stones
of the Pict Wal were pulled down to build Drumbuygh. For the
Wal ys very nere yt.' It is three storeys high with impressive
steps at the western end, and an inscription over the doorway.

After leaving the village the line of the Wall passes through
the hamlet of Glasson south of the coastal road. From the road
there is a fine view north-west over the estuary. Shelduck
and curlew can be seen on the mud at low tide and there
is the frequent call of the oyster-catcher on the shore. As one
approaches Port Carlisle it is possible to cut the corner and
walk along the grass-covered sand-dunes by the edge of the
marshes.

Port Carlisle has a slightly melancholy air, as if only too well
aware of its failure to develop as the maritime outlet of the city
of Carlisle. In 1819 the Earl of Lonsdale constructed a harbour
here and in 1823 a canal was built to provide a link between
Carlisle and the Solway. It cost £90,000 and was 11 miles long
with eight locks. But the completion of the Maryport and
Carlisle Railway in 1845 provided such damaging competition

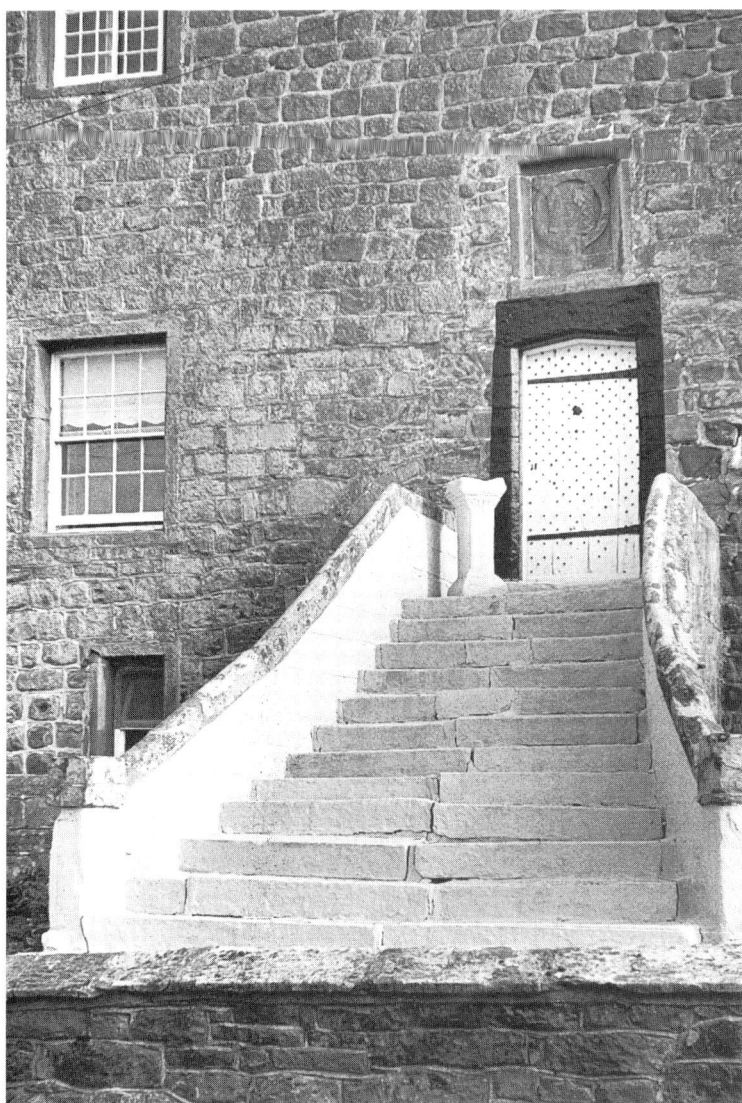

A white-washed Roman altar on the steps of Drumburgh Castle.

that the canal was a financial failure virtually from the start. In 1854 the canal was drained and a railway was laid on its bed. But this venture was also doomed to failure. In 1856 the North British Railway Company built an extension from Drumburgh to Silloth, further down the Cumbrian coast, as a result of which Silloth became the port for Carlisle. The final blow to the commercial success of Port Carlisle came in 1869 when the Caledonian Railway Company built the Solway Junction Railway to carry iron ore from West Cumbria to the furnaces of Lanarkshire. A viaduct was constructed across the Solway from Bowness to Annan, which prevented the passage of any sizeable boat further up the estuary. The viaduct remained in regular use until 1914 and was demolished in 1935. For 50 years after the opening of the Silloth line the Drumburgh to Port Carlisle section was operated by a horse drawn carriage. In April 1914 the line reverted to steam traction and it was finally closed in 1932.

Port Carlisle consists of one street of rather staid Victorian houses facing the sea. The remains of the old station platform can be seen beside the bowling green and parts of the canal basin and harbour works may still be traced. The only sign of the Romans is a small altar built into the wall over the door of Hesket House, formerly the Steam Packet Hotel, at the western end of the village. This was dedicated to the Mother Goddesses and the letters MATRIBUS SUIS may just be discerned. Those who have walked from Carlisle may be glad to see the Hope and Anchor pub.

After leaving the village one may again cut the corner by walking on the edge of Bowness Marsh. In the early 18th century the Wall still stood some ten feet high in this section, but it is sad to note that there are now no traces of anything Roman. Bowness-on-Solway is a quiet little village with steep cobbled streets. It lies just west of the lowest ford on the Solway, a route used by John Wesley in 1766. The Roman fort, known as Maia, was placed on a cliff overlooking the sea and occupied an area of seven acres, making it the second largest fort on the Wall. It was in a position of great strategic importance, guarding the approaches across the Solway. It is hard to find any traces of the fort today. Information about it is given in a notice on the west wall of the King's Arms, an inn which serves

The bell from Dornock, now resting in the porch of St Michael's Church, Bowness-on-Solway.

an excellent Sunday lunch. The only Roman object to be seen in the village is the head of an altar to Jupiter. This may be seen above the lintel of the blocked door of a stable belonging to Bowness House Farm in the main street. The lettering IOM, standing for Iuppiter Optimus Maximus ('Jupiter Greatest and Best'), cannot now be distinguished.

St Michael's Church dates back to Norman times and is built largely of stones from the Wall. The two bells in the porch were taken from the churches of Dornock and Middlebie across the Solway in Scotland. During one of the border raids of the 17th century a group of Scots crossed the Solway by boat and stole the bells of Bowness church. They were pursued by the men of Bowness and to lighten their boat were forced to throw the bells overboard at a spot now known as Bell Pool. In revenge a group of men from Bowness raided the Scottish coast and returned with the bells of Dornock and Middlebie. These bells were in regular use at Bowness until a new pair was donated in 1905.

If you want to say you have been to the end of the Wall you should go to the western end of the village and walk back along the shore. The Wall is said to have run down to the sea somewhere below the village school. Across the Solway the 1868 foot summit of Criffel dominates the western skyline, while to the north are the conspicuous smoke-filled chimneys of Chapple Cross power station. When I was last here I met a resident of the village who told me that at certain conditions of low tide a Roman altar could be seen in the sea. He also said that he had once seen a jogger running across the Solway. Half a mile to the west of the village are the remains of the old railway viaduct across the Firth to Annan. With care one may walk out along the top of the grass-covered embankment to view its rust-covered remains.

Bowness marks the western end of the Wall but it is not the end of the Roman system of surveillance. Excavations in recent years have shown that a series of small forts and towers, but without the accompanying Wall, stretched for a further 40 miles down the Cumbrian coast at least as far as Maryport (where one should visit the recently-opened Senhouse Roman Museum). But for those who have traced the frontier from Wallsend, Bowness marks the end of the pilgrimage along Hadrian's Wall. The frontier has passed through some wild and desolate country and it seems somehow appropriate that it should come to an end at this peaceful spot overlooking the salt flats and lonely waters of the Solway.

# CHAPTER 9

## *Pilgrims on the Wall*

Hadrian's Wall has commanded the attention of scholars and writers for many centuries. Any attempt to describe the activities of those who have made a pilgrimage to the Wall must start with the man responsible for the whole concept, Publius Aelius Hadrianus, the Emperor Hadrian himself.

Hadrian's family came from Spain where he was born in AD 76. His father died when he was nine and he was entrusted to the care of two guardians, one of whom was the future emperor Trajan, a cousin of his father. As a boy Hadrian developed a love of hunting which was to remain with him all his life. He also developed a passionate interest in the Greeks and their culture. After entering the Senate he served as a tribune with Legion II Adiutrix in what is now Yugoslavia. Trajan became emperor in AD 98 and ten years later Hadrian was adopted as his heir.

On Trajan's death in AD 117 Hadrian set himself the task of reviewing the state of the Empire. Under Trajan the policy had been to extend the borders of the Empire but Hadrian wished to pursue a policy of consolidation. He knew the Empire had become too big to control and defend efficiently. He abandoned some of Trajan's recent conquests, such as Assyria and Mesopotamia and then set himself the task of establishing secure frontiers. He went to inspect the frontier on the Lower Danube, and in southern Germany he strengthened the border by a continuous palisade. In AD 122 he came to Britain, where there had been trouble in the north of the province. He was one of the few reigning emperors to visit Britain.

Little is known about Hadrian's movements in Britain. He is said to have travelled without any fuss or splendour, never riding in a litter or wheeled vehicle but always going on foot or riding on horseback. A Roman poet of the time called Florus wrote a witty poem in which he said how sorry he felt for the emperor having to visit far-distant Britain. It has been suggested that the decision to build the Wall was taken

Hadrian, Emperor AD 117–138.

before Hadrian arrived in Britain and that changes to the original plan were made after he had paid a personal visit to the frontier zone.

After leaving Britain Hadrian continued on his travels in the provinces of the empire, spending 13 years of his 21 year reign on such journeys. One important result of his visits to the provinces was a boost in the morale of the provincial people of the empire, and during his reign there was a period of relative peace. He introduced significant administrative, financial and legal reforms and was responsible for some magnificent public buildings. Hadrian died in Italy in AD 138 aged 62.

The earliest known writer to mention the remains of the Wall was the Venerable Bede (AD 673-735). Bede was a monk at the monastery of Jarrow. He described the Wall as being eight feet in breadth and twelve in height. He thought the Vallum was built as an earlier line of defence before the construction of the Wall.

After Bede little is known of the Wall until the time of the great Elizabethan antiquary, William Camden. He was the Headmaster of Westminster School and travelled extensively in Britain. In 1599 he explored most of the Wall on foot and wrote: 'Verily I have seen the tract of it over the high pitches and steepe descents of the hilles, wonderfully rising and falling.' But he did not explore the central section, commenting: 'I could not with safety take the full survey for the rank robbers thereabouts.' An account of his travels was given in the 5th edition of his *Britannia*, which was produced in 1600. Here he expressed the view that the Vallum was the work of Hadrian and that the Wall was built by Severus (emperor AD 193–211). This erroneous view of the dating of the various features of the frontier system was accepted for the next 250 years.

Camden's studies fostered an interest in the Wall amongst later antiquarians. One of the most famous was the Revd John Horsley (1685–1732). He was a Presbyterian minister who ran a private school in Morpeth and was also a Fellow of the Royal Society. His *Britannia Romana* was published after his death in 1732. This work was based on careful and penetrating observation and for many years it remained the standard book on the Wall. Another antiquarian, the Revd William Stukely, also a Fellow of the Royal Society, wrote a work called *Iter*

*Boreale* (Northern Journey) which was published after his death in 1776. This book contains useful drawings showing the state of the ruins in his time.

Probably the most colourful and certainly one of the most unusual pilgrims on the Wall was William Hutton, who in 1801 at the age of 78 set out from his home town of Birmingham, walked through the Lake District to Carlisle, twice covered the length of the Wall and then walked back home, completing a distance of 601 miles in 35 days. Hutton was a successful businessman who had long had a passionate desire to see the Wall. He left home on 4 July 1801 accompanied by his daughter Catherine who rode pillion behind a servant and made all the arrangements for his accommodation. After crossing Morecambe Bay and walking the length of Windermere and Ullswater, he arrived in Penrith on 17 July. Here he parted from his daughter and made his way north to Carlisle. After visiting the western end of the Wall at Bowness on Solway, he returned to Carlisle and walked to Newcastle and on to Wallsend, before going back along the Wall to Carlisle. After returning home Hutton produced his *History of the Roman Wall*, which was first published in 1802. A second edition was produced in 1813, which was accompanied by a letter from his daughter, explaining how he came to carry out this project.

When writing about his epic walk Hutton decided that like his predecessors he would describe a westward journey from Wallsend to Bowness. Setting out from Wallsend, where no remains were to be seen and the site of the fort was a green pasture, he was saddened to note that the Ditch was being levelled to grow potatoes. At Newcastle he dined in the company of seven gentlemen and throughout the meal he could not help noticing a feeling of tension and restraint. It was only when he was asked to say grace afterwards that he realised that his black dress had caused him to be taken for a clergyman. He had a similar experience when he reached Harlow Hill, where three gentlemen sitting in an inn were at first extremely cool, thinking him to be a spy employed by the government. He tells us that on several occasions initial fears over his identity caused him to receive an unfavourable reception. At various times he was taken for a Methodist preacher, a surveyor of land 'preparatory to enclosing the commons', a surveyor of

William Hutton, 1723–1815.

land 'employed by the landlord preparatory to a rise of rent', and 'a person employed by the government to examine private property for the advancement of taxation'!

After visiting the fort of Halton Chesters he reached Portgate, where he was delighted to find a large section of the Vallum surviving in very good condition. Five miles further on, at a spot where there had been a long stretch of Wall rising in places over seven feet high, he found that the owner of the land was taking the Wall down to build a farm house. He had already destroyed nearly 100 yards of Wall. Hutton begged the servant whom he met to tell the owner to desist and added: 'If the Wall was of no estimation, he must have a mean opinion of me, who would travel six hundred miles to see it.'

After crossing the River North Tyne he visited the fort of Chesters and spent the night at the Twice Brewed Inn. The next morning he made his way to the nearby fort of Housesteads, which he described as 'the grandest Station in the whole line'. After exploring the site and commenting on the extensive remains, he concluded: 'It is not easy to survey these important ruins without a sigh: a place once of the greatest activity, but now a solitary desert; instead of the human voice, is heard nothing but the winds.'

At Hare Hill he was delighted to see a portion of the Wall standing ten feet high — the highest he saw on all his journey. As evening was approaching, he went to an inn bearing the sign of the Cow and Boot. Although at first they would not take him in, they relented when he insisted that he had nowhere else to go. The landlord had six daughters, one of whom was very seriously ill. Hutton noted that: 'Although a public-house, they had no ale, cyder, porter, beer, or liquors of any kind, or food, except milk, which was excellent; but they treated me with something preferable, Civility.' On the next day he reached Stanwix, where he had considerable difficulty in securing a bed for the night. After two refusals, he was much put out when he was rejected by a third lady, until he later discovered that she had had an affair with a local duke who still visited her on occasions!

A mile before reaching the end of his quest at Bowness, he came upon a fine section of Wall, five hundred yards long and three feet high, rising to six feet in a few places. When he met a local farmer who expressed pleasure in having destroyed several sections of the Wall, Hutton replied in characteristic fashion, hoping that the next stone he disturbed might break his mattock, and begging him not to touch one more stone until his return. After visiting Bowness and admiring the Scottish coast across the Solway Firth, he retraced his steps to Carlisle and set off southwards to rejoin his daughter at Hest Bank. After resting for four days he began his journey home and reached Birmingham on 7 August. He says he arrived home, 'after a loss, by perspiration, of one stone of animal weight, an expenditure of forty guineas, a lapse of thirty five days, and a walk of six hundred and one miles.'

Another picture of the Wall as it was in 1801 may be obtained from the diary of the Revd John Skinner, the Rector of Camerton in Somerset. In August that year he set out on a five week walking tour in Northumberland and Cumberland, and in the period 11–26 September he walked the whole length of the Wall. He was not very happy about his reception by the locals, remarking that 'civility to strangers by no means appears to be a characteristic of the country people of Northumberland.' On several occasions he thought that the local people were happy for him to be attacked by their dogs before deigning to answer his enquiries! He was most impressed by his visit to Housesteads, commenting: 'Surely there must be as much scope here for the observation of the antiquarian as any spot in the kingdom.' It is exasperating today to read that in the last mile coming into Bowness the Wall was 'very visible being in some parts nearly 6 ft high.' He noted that the Roman cement was so strong that 'this monument of Roman masonry bids fair to remain for ages if it has only the elements to contend with.' Sadly it has had the ravages of man to contend with, and today there are no obvious signs of the Wall in the western sector. On his return from Bowness John Skinner visited the monument to Edward I on the marsh near Burgh and was interested to note that the titles and grandeur of the Duke of Norfolk who erected the monument in 1645 seemed to occupy more space than those of the monarch whom it was commemorating. At the time of Skinner's visit the monument had recently fallen down and was lying in pieces.

John Clayton, 1792–1890.

In 1812 the Revd John Hodgson, the Vicar of Jarrow, published a comprehensive account of the Wall in his *Picture of Newcastle upon Tyne.* He followed this by his *History of Northumberland*, the last volume of which, published in 1839, was largely devoted to the Roman Wall. This work was particularly important because Hodgson showed, on the evidence of inscriptions, that the Wall was built by Hadrian, and not by the later Emperor, Severus.

The man who probably did more than anyone else to preserve the remains of the Wall from destruction was John Clayton (1792–1890) who owned the estate on which lay the fort of Chesters. Clayton was a remarkable man. For nearly 60 years he ran one of the largest legal practices in the north of England and, as Town Clerk of Newcastle from 1822 until 1867, he played a major role in the rebuilding of the city. He was a noted classical scholar and, after excavating the Roman fort of Chesters which lay in front of his house, he devoted himself to the systematic exploration of neighbouring forts, milecastles and turrets. Realising that the survival of the Roman Wall was threatened by local farmers who were using it as a quarry, he tried wherever possible to buy the land over which the Wall ran. On his death he owned five Roman forts, including Housesteads, Chesters and Vindolanda.

No name has been more associated with the Wall and its literature than that of John Collingwood Bruce (1805-1892). Bruce was a graduate of Glasgow University who returned to his native Northumberland as the headmaster of a school in Newcastle. He remained there for the rest of his life, devoting himself to researching and writing on Roman antiquities. He rapidly became the leading authority on the Wall and in 1851 produced his great work *The Roman Wall*. It is a detailed description of the remains of the Wall and contains a large number of line drawings and reproductions of inscriptions.

Bruce's interest in the Wall was stimulated by a visit he made along its length in the summer of 1848 after the current political situation had forced him to cancel a visit to Southern Europe. He took with him his 14 year old son and two local artists Henry and Charles Richardson. The three elder men travelled in an open carriage while his son rode on a pony.

John Collingwood Bruce, 1805–1892.

Bruce returned from this trip with copious notes on the Wall, and the paintings done by the Richardsons now hang in the Laing Gallery in Newcastle. During the winter of 1848–9 Bruce gave a series of lectures on the Roman Wall to the Newcastle Literary and Philosophical Society. Anxious to avoid any impression that he was exaggerating the importance and extent of the remains he suggested that the members of the Society might like to accompany him on a pilgrimage along the whole length of the Wall the following summer. Most of the pilgrims travelled on foot but their baggage was conveyed in a commodious brake, drawn by two horses nicknamed Romulus and Remus. Although they engaged in a little excavation at Greatchesters and at Birdoswald, the occasion was a fairly light-hearted affair and they took as much pleasure in the beauty of the countryside as in the Roman remains.

In the years after 1849 a second pilgrimage was mooted from time to time but nothing came of it until 1886. In that year the Society of Antiquaries of Newcastle joined forces with the Cumberland and Westmorland Antiquarian and Archaeological Society in a pilgrimage which was intended as a tribute to the work of Dr Bruce. Bruce himself, although in his 81st year, was appointed Chief Pilgrim. At several places special excavations were carried out in honour of the occasion. This pilgrimage was a great success and it was decided that similar pilgrimages should be conducted at regular ten year intervals. There was done in 1896 and 1906, but because of the Great War the 5th pilgrimage was delayed until 1920. The 11th pilgrimage was held in 1989.

In 1863 Bruce produced the first edition of what he called *The Wallet Book of the Roman Wall*. This was intended to be a short guide containing essential information for those contemplating a pilgrimage along the Wall. The first edition sold out within a year and in 1884 he produced a second edition, this time more appropriately entitled *Handbook to the Roman Wall*. This edition sold out within a few weeks and in 1885 a third edition was produced. Bruce died in 1892 but a fourth edition of his *Handbook* was produced in 1895 and in the intervening years it has continued to be published and is the work by which Bruce is best known today. It continued the format of describing a traverse of the Wall from east to west and it has always borne Bruce's name. The *Handbook* has been revised by a succession of scholars who have taken account of the latest discoveries. The latest edition available is the 13th, produced in 1978 and edited by Charles Daniels of Newcastle University.

In 1920 the writer and artist, Jessie Mothersole, set out on a pilgrimage along the Wall. She described her experiences in her book, *Hadrian's Wall*, which was produced two years later. This book is interesting not only for the account she gives of the remains of the Wall in the early part of this century, but also for her description of the social conditions in the period immediately after the Great War. Influenced by the example of the intrepid William Hutton, she walked the length of the Wall from east to west.

Jessie Mothersole was a lady of considerable energy. Arriving in Newcastle on the night train from King's Cross at 5 am on her first day, she thought nothing of walking immediately to Wallsend, and then setting out eastwards through Newcastle to East Wallhouses to spend her first night in a house near the Robin Hood Inn, a journey of over 20 miles, much of it in a temperature of 81 degrees in the shade. At Wallsend she was amused to see an old woman in a dirty apron and grey shawl going round and knocking at ground floor windows with a small hammer, and crying: 'Lizzie, it's well nigh six o'clock' and 'Mary, it's time ye riz.' This was her first sight of a 'knocker-up'. In Throckley she met striking miners, dressed in their best Sunday clothes in order to attend a neighbour's funeral. At Portgate she called at the Errington Arms for a glass of milk and found the postman reclining on a window-seat in a Panama hat and carpet slippers, reading a newspaper. When her drink arrived she found she had no change to pay the bill. As she was about to go and was looking for some money the postman quietly told her that he had settled her account. She records that it was her first experience of being 'treated' in a public house. On this and on other occasions Miss Mothersole had a quite different experience from that of John Skinner who had distrusted the locals so much in 1801.

Jessie Mothersole was examining the Vallum a couple of miles west of Portgate when she suddenly noticed a gorse bush on fire. Breaking off some green boughs of elder she started to beat the fire out, but it took half an hour's effort before she was satisfied the fire was dead. After examining the Chesters bridge abutment she found the waters of the North Tyne so low and placid that she took off her shoes and stockings and entered the bed of the river. It was not long before she found the two piers of the bridge in the river with their pointed ends facing up-stream. She crossed to the Chesters side of the river but then, overcome by conscience at not having paid her entrance fee, she continued along the west bank of the river to enjoy tea at the George at Chollerford.

Not even Jessie Mothersole could persuade the Twice Brewed Inn to provide her with tea, but she found a farm nearby where she stayed for a few days while she did her sketching. The husband was a miner who worked on night shifts and she used to get up early to share his meal when he returned home at five o'clock in the morning. On one long June day she started for the Wall at 5.30 am and did not return till 10 pm. She used to cycle along the military road and leave her bicycle at a farm near where she wished to sketch. At one farm she was amused to see a horse looking in at a bedroom window from which a voice was calling: 'I'm a-coming; I'm a-coming.' Presently an old lady appeared and explained that the horse always looked for his corn at half-past six sharp.

Miss Mothersole always seemed to be able to find a farmhouse which would provide her with a huge tea. On one day she cycled through Caw Gap to the hamlet of Edges Green to make a sketch of Winshields Crags. She had no sooner finished than thunder and heavy rain forced her to take shelter at the nearest house. After apologising for having nothing in the house to give her for tea, the farmer's wife treated her to an abundant spread of cheese, jam, scones, white and brown bread, and two kinds of cake. When she sought to make payment, she was told: 'Oh, it's nothin; it's just a drink o' tea.' On another occasion after passing through Greatchesters, a heavy rain storm forced her to take shelter at Allolee farmhouse, where she was hospitably received. Her clothes were hung up to dry and she was fed to her heart's content.

When she reached the River Irthing, Jessie Mothersole had no trouble fording the river and climbing the steep bank up to the fort at Birdoswald. On another occasion she saw a girl crossing the river in a little wooden chair suspended from a wire, pulling herself across by another wire. After making enquiries she found it belonged to the neighbouring farm of Underheugh and having obtained permission she crossed the river on several occasions in this primitive chair. She said it felt funny being suspended from a rope over the middle of the Irthing. At the end of her stay on the Wall Jessie Mothersole was delighted to be allowed to join the three day joint Pilgrimage of the Society of Antiquaries of Newcastle upon Tyne and the Cumberland and Westmorland Archaeological Society which took place in September 1920.

A picture of the Wall in the 1950's is given by David Harrison, who walked its length in 1954 and wrote of his experiences in his book *Along Hadrian's Wall* published in 1956. His book is very well researched and is a mine of information about the Wall and its system, but you need Latin to understand some of his quotations! He started his pilgrimage in atrocious weather. That summer was the worst for fifty years and on his first few days he had to encounter incessant rain. After a long day's walk from Heddon on the Wall he too enjoyed the hospitality of the Robin Hood Inn at East Wallhouses. When he reached Twice Brewed he stayed at the Bognor Guest-House (now the Vallum Lodge Hotel) and enjoyed the customary large 'plain tea', consisting of toasted tea cake, white and brown bread and butter with crab apple jelly, home-made cakes and a slice of apple pie. He was fortunate to meet Dr D. J. Smith who was conducting excavations at Housesteads and was also staying in the guest house. After visiting Housesteads and walking along the Wall to Greatchesters, David Harrison was delighted to find on returning to the guest house that Dr Smith was entertaining Professor Ian Richmond, the great authority on the Wall who was later to edit the twelfth edition of Bruce's *Handbook*. Harrison learned a great deal from the hour he spent with Ian Richmond and was impressed by his enthusiasm for the Wall and its history.

On reaching the Willowford bridge abutment beside the Irthing David Harrison rose to the challenge and, discarding shoes and socks and rolling up his trousers, he waded across the river and climbed the steep cliffs to the Harrow Scar Milecastle and the fort at Birdoswald. He also visited the Coombe Crag quarry west of Birdoswald, where he was thrilled to find that there were still some traces of the names of Roman soldiers. At the Black Bull in the village of Walton he enjoyed another fine 'plain tea' of which the highlight was a flat gooseberry tart made of the smallest berries he had ever seen.

After arriving in Carlisle and visiting the Tullie House Museum the weather was so cold, although it was the end of June, that he took refuge in a cinema where he had to sit through a highly romantic version of the Japanese attack on Pearl Harbor in December 1941. He compensated for this experience by giving himself a dinner of roast goose and fresh strawberries and retired to bed early before his final day's walk to Bowness. His luck was in and even in remote Bowness he found a friendly farmer who insisted on giving him tea!

In 1974 Hunter Davies produced his book *A Walk along the Wall*, based on a year he spent in Wall country visiting the major sites and talking to some of the people who lived in the area. This is the most varied and interesting of all the books on the Wall. During his researches Hunter Davies walked the length of the Wall, taking a special interest in the people he met and in the problems of landowners and others who control the environment of the Wall country. At Chesters he visited the owner of the estate, Major John Benson, with whom he discussed the problems of the large numbers of visitors to the fort. Occasionally gates were left open and grazing cattle came to harm. One cow had died through eating the leaves of a yew tree after straying amongst the trees. At Housesteads in conditions of high wind and driving rain he came across Valerie Singleton and the BBC Blue Peter team desperately trying to defeat the weather. They made several attempts to ignore the conditions, until the cameraman suddenly slipped in the mud and disappeared down a muddy slope together with his camera.

At Hexham Hunter Davies called on Eric Birley, former Professor of Archaeology at Durham University, and the greatest living authority on the Wall. He heard how in 1929 Eric Birley had bought Chesterholm and the neighbouring farm which contained the fort of Vindolanda. During the war he had served in military intelligence and, using the same methods by which he had assessed the strength of the Roman auxiliary troops in Britain, he had arrived at an amazingly accurate estimate of the size of the German army and was able to provide vital information which assisted the planning of D Day. Davies also had lunch with Eric's son Robin, who is now the Director of the Vindolanda Trust and has been responsible for the remarkable excavations there since 1973. Robin told him of the local opposition they had to overcome because of the large crowds they were beginning to attract to Vindolanda. He also stressed the educational side of their work. Regular courses were arranged for school children who stayed at the nearby Once Brewed Youth Hostel. The children spent half the time in classroom sessions and the other half assisting with current excavations.

Hunter Davies was pleased to return to his teenage roots by staying at the Once Brewed Youth Hostel. Chatting to the warden and his wife he found that in 1973 they served 1300 meals and booked 10,530 bed nights. At Greatchesters he met the tenant farmer who was also a local councillor. He was very critical of the activities of the Vindolanda Trust which were bringing more people to the Wall. He considered that the most important activity in the area was farming and that the Wall should come second.

Davies enjoyed a lengthy conversation with Charles Anderson, the foreman of the team of 30 workmen, 10 masons and 20 labourers, employed by the Department of the Environment. He had been working on the Wall since 1935, caring for the exposed portions and continually unearthing new sections. Davies watched the men at work as they unearthed a large section of the Wall. After clearing the Wall from the mound of earth surrounding it, they cleaned, washed and numbered each stone and laid them out in the order they had come from the Wall. Then, after creating a new inner core of sand and cement and broken stones, they built the Wall up again, carefully placing the facing stones back in their original order. One thing that particularly puzzled Charles Anderson was that in all his years of working on the Wall he had never found a Roman trowel, hammer or mason's tool in the remains.

When skirting round Carlisle Airport Davies had an animated conversation with an old man who turned out to be a molecatcher. He told Davies that before the war he could get a shilling for each mole skin. The price had now fallen so far that it was no longer worth the effort, but he had a contract with local farmers to keep down moles by poison. In Carlisle Davies spoke to Robin Hogg the Curator of the Tullie House Museum. He had worked at Tullie House since leaving school at the age of 16 in 1926. In 1930 he had been detailed to assist the great Roman archaeologist, F. G. Simpson, in his excavations at Stanwix and from this experience stemmed his interest in the Wall. Since that time he had been involved in many excavations in other parts of Cumberland, and it was his excavation which had uncovered the Roman shrine in the gardens of Tullie House.

While in Carlisle Hunter Davies asked the local office of the building firm John Laing to estimate the cost, at 1974 prices, of building the Roman Wall to its original dimensions in concrete. After much calculation the firm estimated that to build the Wall completely to the original Roman plan, to the same width and height and using the same design, would cost £80 million. When this figure is considered in relation to other government spending some idea may be gained of the great burden on Roman military finances which the building of the Wall must have imposed.

Today visitors come to the Wall in ever increasing numbers, drawn by the compelling attraction of this magnificent monument set in countryside of such wild and lonely splendour. No one is likely to exceed the enthusiasm of William Hutton who, as he says, 'at seventy-eight walked six hundred miles to see a shattered Wall'. But Hutton was wrong when he voiced the opinion that after being the first to walk the length of the Wall he would be the last to attempt it. An ever growing number of pilgrims are now following in his footsteps. But those who do embark on this pilgrimage will never be able to express their feelings of admiration for the mighty achievement of the Roman Wall more powerfully than the old man himself: 'I was fascinated and unable to proceed; forgot I was upon a wild common, a stranger and the evening approaching. I had the grandest works under my eye, of the greatest men of the age in which they lived, and of the most eminent nation then existing. . . . Even hunger and fatigue were lost in the grandeur before me. . . . Lost in astonishment, I was not able to move at all.'

# INFORMATION FOR VISITORS

## Museums

These open at 10.00 am unless otherwise stated. Closing times vary according to the time of year and should be checked.

*South Shields Roman Fort* (091 454 4093)
Closed Mondays
Open Sundays 2.00–5.00 pm (Easter to September)
No charge

*Wallsend Heritage Centre* (091 262 2627)
Open 10.30 am Thursdays and Saturdays (from June to October)
No charge

*Newcastle, Museum of Antiquities* (0632 21727)
Open weekdays
No charge

*Corbridge Roman Site* (0434 632349)
Open daily (April to September)
Closed Mondays (October to March)
Admission charge

*Chesters Roman Fort* (0434 681379)
Open daily
Admission charge

*Housesteads Roman Fort* (0434 344363)
Open daily
Admission charge

*Vindolanda* (0434 344277)
Open daily (mid-February to October)
Weekends only (November and early February)
Closed December and January
Admission charge

*Carvoran, Roman Army Museum* (06972 485)
Open daily (March to October)
Weekends only (November and February)
Closed December and January
Admission charge

*Birdoswald* (06977 47602)
    Open 9.30 am (mid-March to October)
    Visits in winter by prior arrangement
    Admission charge
*Carlisle, Tullie House* (0228 34781)
    Open daily throughout the year
    Admission charge

## Best Places to view Remains of the Wall System

| *The Wall* | *Forts* |
|---|---|
| Heddon-on-the-Wall | South Shields |
| Black Carts | Chesters |
| Planetrees | Housesteads |
| Housesteads to Steel Rigg | Vindolanda |
| Cawfield Crags | Birdoswald |
| Walltown Crags | |
| Gilsland to Willowford | |
| Birdoswald | |

| *Milecastles* | *Turrets* |
|---|---|
| MC 37 (Housesteads) | Denton Turret (7b) |
| MC 39 (Castle Nick) | Brunton Turret (26b) |
| MC 42 (Cawfields) | Banks Turret (52a) |
| MC 48 (Poltross Burn) | |
| MC 49 (Harrow's Scar) | |

| *The Vallum* | *The Ditch* |
|---|---|
| Benwell Vallum Crossing | East Wallhouses |
| Limestone Corner | Limestone Corner |
| Sewingshields | |
| Cawfields | |

| *Bridges* | *Temples* |
|---|---|
| Chesters Bridge Abutment | Benwell, Temple of Antenociticus |
| Willowford Bridge Abutment | Carrawburgh, Temple of Mithras |

## Tourist Information Offices

*South Shields* (091 454 6612)

> Museum and Art Gallery
> South Shields
> Tyne and Wear
> NE33 2HZ

*Newcastle* (091 261 0691)

> Central Library
> Princess street
> Newcastle upon Tyne
> NE99 1DX

*Corbridge* (0434 632815)

> Vicar's Pele
> Market Place
> Corbridge
> Northumberland
> NE45 5AW

*Hexham* (0434 605225)

> The Manor Office
> Hallgate
> Hexham
> Northumberland
> NE46 1XD

*Once Brewed* (0434 344396)

> National Park Information
>    Centre
> Once Brewed
> Military Road
> Bardon Mill
> Northumberland
> NE47 7AN

*Haltwhistle* (0434 302351)

> Sycamore Street
> Haltwhistle
> Northumberland
> NE49 0AG

*Brampton* (06977 3433)

> The Moot Hall
> Brampton
> Cumbria
> CA8 1RA

*Carlisle* (0228 512444)

> Old Town Hall
> Green Market
> Carlisle
> Cumbria
> CA3 8JH

## Transport

There is a regular train service between Newcastle and Carlisle with stations at Corbridge, Hexham, Haydon Bridge, Bardon Mill, Haltwhistle and Brampton. In late July and August there is a daily coach service from Hexham to Haltwhistle which runs along the Military Road and is well advertised locally.

## Accommodation

A booklet *Hadrian's Wall Country,* giving details of bed and breakfast and self-catering establishments may be obtained from Tourist Information Offices. Details of Hadrian's Wall Farm Holidays may be obtained from Mrs Sheila Stobbart, Hullerbank, Brampton, Cumbria CA8 1LB (06967 6668).

## Maps

Four Ordnance Survey Landranger 1:50,000 maps are required to cover the whole length of Hadrian's Wall:

88  Tyneside & Durham area
87  Hexham, Haltwhistle & surrounding area
86  Haltwhistle, Bewcastle & Alston area
85  Carlisle & The Solway Firth

Visitors wishing to purchase only one map should buy 86 Haltwhistle, Bewcastle and Alston area, which covers all the central section of the Wall from Sewingshields to beyond Birdoswald.

The Ordnance survey have also produced an historical map and guide, *Hadrian's Wall.* This covers selected areas at $2\frac{1}{2}$ inches to 1 mile.

# Further Reading

Birley, Robin (1990) *Hadrian's Wall : A Personal Guide* (Roman Army Museum)

Breeze, David J and Dobson, Brian (1987) *Hadrian's Wall* 3rd edition (Penguin)

Bruce, J Collingwood (1978) *Handbook to the Roman Wall* 13th edition edited and enlarged by Charles Daniels (Harold Hill)

Davies, Hunter (1974) *A Walk along the Wall* Weidenfeld and Nicolson)

English Heritage (1989) *Hadrian's Wall: A souvenir guide*

Emberton, Ronald and Frank Graham (1990) *Hadrian's Wall in the days of the Romans* (Frank Graham)

Harrison, David (1956) *Along Hadrian's Wall* (Cassell)

Johnson, Stephen (1989) *Hadrian's Wall* (Batsford)

Mothersole, Jessie (1922) *Hadrian's Wall* (Bodley Head)

National Trust (1990) *Hadrian's Wall : An illustrated souvenir*

Northumberland National Park (1982) *Look Around Hadrian's Wall*

Northumberland National Park (1990) *Walks in the Hadrian's Wall area* 3rd edition

Les Turnbull (1974) *Hadrian's Wall Guide Books 1–4* (Harold Hill)

Hutton, William (1813) *The History of the Roman Wall* 1990 reprint (Frank Graham) under title *The First Man to Walk Hadrian's Wall 1802*

Rowland, T. H. (1991) *A Short Guide to the Roman Wall* (Butler Publishing)

Skinner, John (1978) *Hadrian's Wall in 1801* edited by Howard and Peter Coombs (Kingsmead Press)

Thornton, David *The Picture Story of Hadrian's Wall* (D & J Thornton)

# Index

Agricola, governor, 1
Alnwick Castle, 13
Anderson, Charles, 154
Annan, 136, 138
*Antonine Itinerary*, 13
auxiliary troops, 4, 14–15, 18, 23,
24–5, 30, 35, 39, 41, 56, 70, 75,
90, 93–94, 104, 123

Barcombe, 85, 94–6
Beaumont, 130–1
Bede, Venerable, 141
Benwell, 9, 30, 34–6
Bewcastle, 14, 117–9
Birdoswald, 4, 109, 110–3, 117, 149,
151, 152
Birley, Eric, 153–4
Birley, Robin, 89, 154
Birrens, 14, 129
Black Carts, 63, 64
Bowness-on-Solway, 3, 5, 14, 136–8,
144–5, 153
bridges, 13–14, 28, 29, 32, 33, 46,
48, 53–5, 58, 107–9, 123, 129, 151
Broad Wall, 6, 36, 39, 52, 53, 68, 77
Bulmer, William, 30
Burgh-by-Sands, 116, 131–4, 145

Caerleon, 15
Caldew, River, 123, 129
Cam Beck, 121–2
Camden, William, 123, 141
Carlisle, 1, 4, 13, 39, 44, 46–8, 116,
122–9, 153
airport, 122, 154
Castle, 123, 124, 126, 129
Cathedral, 125, 126
St Cuthbert's Church, 125–6
Tullie House Museum, 123, 127–9,
155
Carrawburgh, 30, 31, 61, 64–7, 99
Carvoran Roman Army Museum,
103, 104–5
Castle Nick, 82, 83
Castlesteads, 121

Caw Gap, 97, 99
Cawfield Crags, 97, 98, 100
centurial stones, 68, 107, 110, 115,
119, 123
centuries, 11, 15, 71
Chester, 14, 15
Chesters, 10, 12, 20, 30, 55–62, 67,
153
Chesters Bridge Abutment, 13, 53–5,
58, 151
Chineley Burn, 85, 90, 95
Chollerford, 52, 55, 151
Chollerton, 55
civilian settlements, 12, 75–6, 86–8,
111
Claudius, emperor, 1
Clayton, John, 60–1, 66, 67, 77, 97,
146, 147
Collingwood, Admiral Lord, 21–2,
32
Corbridge, 1, 13, 44–8, 94, 95
Crag Lough, 79, 80, 81
Criffel, 138
Cuthbert, St, 77, 123
Collingwood Bruce, John, 20, 27, 33,
36, 40, 147–50
Cuddy's Crags, 77, 78, 83
Cumbria Coastal Way, 130

Daniels, Charles, 150
Davies, Hunter, 153–5
Denton Burn, 34, 36
Dere Street, 42, 44, 48
Ditch, 4, 7, 15, 38, 39, 41, 50, 52,
63–4, 65, 68, 96, 99, 101, 113–4,
119
Dobson, John, 30, 33
Drumburgh, 134, 135
Dornock, 137

Eden, River, 13, 123, 129, 130
Edward I, 116, 133, 145
English Heritage, 56, 69, 70, 76, 86,
121

161

forts, 4, 5, 6, 9–13, 14, 104
  aqueducts, 44, 56, 72
  barrack blocks, 11–12, 58, 71–2,
    104, 111
  bath houses, 11, 30, 57–8, 86, 87
  commanding officer's houses,
    10–11, 26, 30, 60, 75
  granaries, 11, 23, 26, 44, 45, 71,
    104, 110–12
  headquarters buildings, 10, 20, 26,
    30, 45, 59–60, 74–5, 90, 104, 110
  hospitals, 12, 75
  latrines, 26, 58, 72–3, 86, 87–8, 90
  outpost forts, 4, 14–15, 42, 117
  ovens, 56, 107, 110, 111
  stables, 11
  strong-rooms, 10, 20, 26, 59–60,
    90, 101
Fosse Way, 1

Gilsland, 107–9
Grainger, Richard, 30
Greatchesters, 99–101, 149, 151, 154
Greenhead, 106
Grindsdale, 130, 131

Hadrian, emperor, 1–2, 3, 6,
  139–141, 147
Halton Chesters, 41
Halton Tower, 41–2
Haltwhistle, 106
Haltwhistle Burn, 97
Hare Hill, 119, 120, 144
Harlow Hill, 39, 40, 142
Harrison, David, 152–3
Heavenfield, 50–2
Heddon-on-the-Wall, 38–9
Hexham, 48–9
High Rochester, 14, 42–3
Highshield Crags, 79, 81, 84
Hodgson, Revd John, 147
Hogg, Robin, 155
Horsley, John, 18, 141
Hotbank Crags, 6, 79, 80
Housesteads, 30, 31, 61, 68, 69–76,
  80, 83, 95, 144, 145, 152
Hutton, William, 40, 52, 142–5, 155

inscriptions, 6, 15, 43, 45, 61, 68, 80,
  107, 110, 115, 119, 123, 136, 137
Intermediate Wall, 7
Irthing, River, 5, 13–14, 107–9, 113,
  114, 115, 151–2

Jarrow, 18, 141, 147

Knag Burn gateway, 69

Lanercost Priory, 110, 115–7
legions, 5, 6, 8, 14, 15, 30, 104
  Second Augusta, 6, 8, 15, 77, 80,
    97
  Sixth Victrix, 8, 15, 29, 44, 115
  Twentieth Valeria, 8, 15, 44
Leland, John, 134
Limestone corner, 63–5
lime kilns, 79, 83, 85

Maiden Way, 104, 117
Maryport, 138
*Mauretania*, 17, 18, 20
Middlebie, 137
milecastles, 3, 5, 7–8, 30, 89, 104
  Milecastle 35 (Sewingshields), 69
  Milecastle 37 (Housesteads), 76,
    77, 84
  Milecastle 38 (Hotbank), 6, 79–80
  Milecastle 39 (Castle Nick), 82
  Milecastle 42 (Cawfields), 97, 99,
    100
  Milecastle 48 (Poltross Burn), 107
  Milecastle 49 (Harrow's Scar), 109
milefortlets, 14, 138
Mithraism, 30, 31, 61, 66–7, 75
Military Road (B6318), 4, 39, 41, 42,
  51, 80, 85, 106
Military Way, 4, 6, 8, 9, 14, 54, 72,
  77, 80, 83–4, 109
Milking Gap, 79, 84, 85
models, 7, 8, 10, 24–5, 30–1, 46, 61,
  70, 104
Mothersole, Jessie, 40, 150–2

Narrow Wall, 5, 6, 19, 68, 77, 107
National Trust, 69
Netherby, 14, 129
Newcastle, 4, 5, 17, 23, 27, 28–34,
  39, 142, 147
  bridges, 28, 29
  Museum of Antiquities, 8, 29,
    30–1, 35, 66–7, 80, 101
  Cathedral, 30, 32–3
  Laing Art Gallery, 30
  Castle, 30, 32
  city walls, 30, 33
Nine Nicks of Thirlwell, 101, 103
North Shields, 21, 22

North Tyne, River, 13, 52, 53–5, 63
Northumberland National Park, 63, 85
*Notitia Dignitatum*, 12–13

Onnn Drawed, 05, 06, 151

Peel Crags, 82, 83, 84
Peel Gap, 83, 85, 96
peel towers, 46, 106, 112, 113, 125
Pennine Way, 77, 83, 96, 106
Pike Hill, signal tower, 101, 114
Planetrees, 5, 52
Platorius Nepos, Aulus, governor, 6
Port Carlisle, 134–6
Portgate, 42, 144, 150

Rapishaw Gap, 77, 79, 83
*Ravenna List*, 13
reconstructions, 19, 23–6, 86, 88–9, 92, 95, 103, 104
Rede, River, 42, 43
Richardson, Charles, 30, 147
Richardson, Henry, 30, 112, 147
Richmond, Sir Ian, 26, 152
Risingham, 14, 42, 43
Robin Hood Inn, 40, 150, 152
Rudchester, 39, 41
*Rudge Cup*, 13

Scotland, 1, 9, 23
Severus, emperor, 141, 147
Sewingshields Crags, 68, 69
Simpson, F. G., 19, 82, 96, 155
Skiddaw, 114, 131
Skinner, Revd John, 145, 150
Smith, Dr D. J., 152
Solway Firth, 1, 2, 5, 106, 131, 134, 136, 138
South Shields, 21, 23–7, 105
St Bees, 14
Stanegate, 1, 5, 44, 80, 85, 86, 90, 91, 95, 103
Stanwix, 123, 144, 155
Steel Rigg, 81, 83, 96
Stephenson, George, 33, 72
Stephenson, Robert, 29
Stukely, William, 27, 141–2

Swan Hunter, shipyard, 17, 19, 20
Sycamore Gap, 81, 83, 84

Thirlwall Castle, 106
Tipalt Burn, 104, 106
Trajan, emperor, 1, 139
Turf Wall, 7, 8, 89, 110, 114
turrets, 3, 5, 6, 8, 30, 55, 68, 69, 71, 82, 88
Turret 7b (Denton), 36–7
Turret 26b (Brunton), 52–3
Turret 29a (Black Carts), 63
Turret 33b (Coesike), 68
Turret 44b (Mucklebank), 101
Turret 45a (Walltown), 101
Turret 48a (Willowford), 107
Turret 51a (Piper Sike), 114
Turret 51b (Leahill), 114
Turret 52a (Banks), 114
Twice Brewed Inn, 85, 144, 151
Tyne, River, 1, 2, 5, 17, 20, 21, 22, 25–6, 28, 30, 37
Tyne and Wear Museums Service, 26, 58
Tynemouth, 18, 20–2

Vallum, 4, 6, 8–9, 28, 34, 39, 41, 50, 63, 64, 68, 97, 100, 114, 130, 141, 144
Vallum crossing, 9, 30, 35–6
Vindolanda, 12, 20, 80, 85–96, 104, 153, 154
Vindolanda Trust, 86, 104, 154

Wade, General, 4
Wallsend, 3, 6, 17–20, 24, 27, 30, 142, 150
Walltown Crags, 2, 101–3, 106
Walton, 119, 121, 153
Walwick, 63
Wark Forest, 77
Whin Sill, 4, 16, 67–8, 106
Wilfrid, St, 48
Willowford Bridge Abutment, 13, 107–9
Wilmot, Tony, 113
Winshields Crags, 96, 151

York, 14, 15, 42